Breaking Down Breaking Bad

Breaking Down Breaking Bad

Unpeeling the Layers of Television's Greatest Drama

By Eric San Juan

Published in the United States of America
By Eric San Juan
ericsanjuan@gmail.com
http://www.ericsanjuan.com

First printing, November 2013

Cover illustration by Rick Lundeen.
Cover design by Eric San Juan and Brian Spaeth.

TABLE OF CONTENTS

ACKNOWLEDGEMENTS

This book could not have happened without a few important people. Thanks to Jim McDevitt for introducing me to *Breaking Bad* in the first place and for your generous proofreading. Your efforts made this book immeasurably better. Thanks to Rick Lundeen for getting me fired up about discussing Walter White's adventures, for your thoughtful input, and of course, for the fantastic cover illustration. This book looks great thanks to you! The prolific and creative Brian Spaeth provided valuable input on the cover design, but more importantly, valuable inspiration when it came to pursuing a project like this in the first place. Thank you for the idea thoughts you are making happen in my head. And of course, the entire gang at the Refuge – you know who you are – unwittingly provided the spark that became *Breaking Down Breaking Bad*. Thanks for that.

But most of all, thanks to Vince Gilligan, Bryan Cranston, Aaron Paul and the rest of the *Breaking Bad* team for creating something so wonderful. We were blessed to be allowed into the world you created.

INTRODUCTION

I can't claim to love television. If it weren't for some key shows, I'd be one of those obnoxious people who say, "I don't watch TV," and the statement would be largely accurate. I don't enjoy pissing away the hours flipping through channels and settling on viewing something good enough to kill an hour but not good enough to make me call my friends and say, "Did you SEE that?" I also hate having an appointment with the television. I hate having my schedule dictated by a show. "Thursdays at 10pm I am on the couch because X is on" is not for me.

Yet once in a great while, something comes along that serves as a Siren call, a flashing beacon in the foggy distance that says, "Sail your ship over here!" and puts my ass in front of the screen at a prescribed time on a prescribed night. Or, more often, has me blitzing through a marathon of TV two and three and four episodes a night, every night, because I just can't turn away.

Breaking Bad is one of those shows.

Like *Deadwood*, like *The Sopranos*, like *The Wire*, this was a show that grabbed me quickly and kept me watching, yet was also something more than mere entertainment. After all, *Mad Men*, *Dexter*, *Rome* and other shows also had me pushing through episode after episode, too, but I never felt as if I was watching something that would last for the ages with those shows; something I'd be able to unpeel layer upon layer, exploring depths that went beyond the drama of the surface narrative.

This show did that. Something about Walter White's struggle not just with the deep waters he had plunged himself into, but with the corners of himself he had never explored before, resonated with me. The idea that his foray into meth production was not merely a dalliance with darkness, but was a full-blown *awakening* for Walt intrigued me.

And most of all, the idea that I actually came to loathe the protagonist of my favorite show utterly fascinated me from a storytelling point of view. How on Earth did these writers make me want to watch this guy every week when I had almost nothing good to say about him as a person?

Yet they managed the trick.

Some years ago, with the help of my friend and collaborator Jim McDevitt, I threw myself into the darkness that was the work of Alfred Hitchcock with *A Year of Hitchcock: 52 Weeks with the Master of Suspense* (Scarecrow Press 2009), unraveling what made him tick as a creator of dark and nasty deeds, then later plunged into the black heart of his evil doers with *Hitchcock's Villains: Murderers, Maniacs and Mother Issues* (Scarecrow Press 2013), a foray into some of the ugliest minds ever to appear on screen.

With *Breaking Down Breaking Bad*, I attempt to do the same, poking into the dark corners of Walter White's mind, exploring the traits that make this show special, and generally reveling in the joy that is arguably the best drama ever to appear on television.

I hope you'll enjoy taking the ride with me.

Eric San Juan
September 2013

WHAT THE HELL IS THIS SHOW, ANYWAY?

What is *Breaking Bad*? The question is a big one or a small one depending on how deep you want get into things. On the surface it's rather simple. You know the pitch by now: A high school chemistry teacher discovers he has incurable cancer, and in an effort to provide for his family starts to cook meth, becoming a "bad guy" in the process.

"I originally pitched it to the studio with one line," creator Vince Gilligan told *The Guardian*. "I told them: 'This is a story about a man who transforms himself from Mr Chips into Scarface.'" (1)

It's a good elevator pitch, really, even though Gilligan wasn't entirely sure how viable the concept would be. That's understandable. After all, what do you *do* with a concept like that? We know now, of course, but it's the sort of pitch that could easily have been spun into a fairly shallow show about a seemingly ordinary guy who manufactures drugs. Crime shows are a dime a dozen, after all, and few of them are any good.

So yes, *Breaking Bad* is about a high school chemistry teacher who discovers he has incurable cancer and, in an effort to provide for his family, starts to cook meth, becoming a "bad guy" in the process. It sounds a bit offbeat, and it is. Yet it works. The show often veers back and forth between black comedy and straight drama, and does so with ease. It's brilliantly written (even the most absurd turns feel totally natural), stunningly acted (Bryan Cranston, also known for playing the dad on *Malcolm in the Middle*, won three straight Emmy's for his performance as Walter White and may win a fourth after this book goes to press), and impossibly gripping (the cut to black at the end of each episode leaves you begging for more).

But it's much more than great acting and sharp entertainment. Strip away the surface trappings and *Breaking Bad* becomes a show about *us*; a show about you and me. It's an exploration of the dark places people will go to and the reasons they will go there. We don't notice it because we are so engrossed in the story, but the questions it grapples with grow larger and more difficult to answer by the episode. Even at their most basic they turn our stomach in increasingly complex knots:

Would you engage in minor illegal activity to provide for your family? Perhaps. It's a twist on the old notion of stealing a loaf of bread in order to survive, and most people (though certainly not all) feel that such a transgression is minor if survival is on the line.

Would you do something pretty damn illegal but that harms no one (as far as you know) to help your loved ones, knowing it will provide for them forever? Long-term security is difficult to come by, after all, especially for an aging schlep with no good future prospects. As long as no one is being harmed …

Would you kill if it meant protecting your own life, knowing your death means your efforts to provide for your loved ones will die with you? Cold-blooded murder is not something most of us would contemplate, but maybe if we look at this from the right angle we'll see this would just be a matter of self-defense.

Would you kill if it meant protecting the life of someone important to you, a person essential to your efforts to provide for your loved ones? Okay, maybe this takes a step or two past self-defense, but viewed through a funhouse mirror this is really just an extension of protecting and providing for your family, right? Or maybe not. Maybe we've strayed too far down the path to see clearly. Maybe we're no longer seeing just how questionable our actions really are. We thought we were just going to wade into ankle-deep water and now we're in mud up to our hips, unable to get out.

And so on until we've reached places even the most unsavory of us wouldn't go. (Poisoning children, anyone?) Most of these questions seem a bit obvious, and our line – the place where we would all throw in the towel and say "I can't do bad things to accomplish good anymore!" – differs, but grappling with the questions can be fun.

Yet the show delves even deeper than merely grappling with simple moral questions. Before we realize it's happening, *Breaking Bad* becomes a character study the likes of which has rarely been seen on television. Perhaps *All In The Family's* Archie Bunker provided depths such as this. Maybe *Deadwood's* Al Swearengen. Certainly Tony Soprano of *The Sopranos.* There are a handful of other television characters you can name who can be explored to the depths we can explore Walter White, but they are few, and in many cases the depth is an illusion.

Take, for instance, *Dexter*, a show that reached its climax at the same time as *Breaking Bad* (which is part of the reason why many commentators, fairly or unfairly, choose the comparison). This is a series about a serial killer trained only to kill those who "deserve" to die; murderers, rapists, and so on. The titular character copes with his impulse to kill by targeting only "bad" people, and over the course of the series must come to grips with his inability to feel emotions and love. It lasted eight seasons. A run that long certainly suggests a good measure of success. One would assume that over the course of those eight seasons we'd explore the difficult question of whether evil deeds can accomplish good things, and whether people who do harm to others can be redeemed if their intensions are noble.

If *Dexter* sounds like ripe material for deep character exploration, however, it's not. The creators opted to take a fascinating premise and use it primarily for surface-level drama and entertainment. They failed to truly explore the depths of who and what the titular is, focusing instead on soap opera drama and boilerplate thrills. There is nothing wrong with that, of course. The show entertained a devoted group of fans (including this author) and won a loyal following. And when it comes down to it, that's the goal of all television shows. To entertain.

But *Breaking Bad* and its main character, Walter White, is a much different puzzle to unravel, and one ultimately more rewarding to delve into. Walter shows us how far we will go for what is important to us and, more importantly, teaches us that the things we think are important to us are often lies we tell ourselves in order to justify the things we do. It peels back the layers of who we really are, what we really desire, and what we would really do to be who we've always secretly aspired to be.

And as we'll explore in the chapters ahead, those secret aspirations can be rather selfish and ugly.

1) The Guardian, "Breaking Bad creator Vince Gilligan: The man who turned Walter White from Mr. Chips into Scarface," May 18, 2012

BREAKING DOWN SEASON 1

On January 20, 2008, television changed forever. We didn't know it at the time. We had no way of knowing it. But wheels had been set into motion that would forever change the way we judge television dramas.

It was hard not to be drawn in from the start. The show opens with a man in "tighty whitey" underwear and a gas mask driving a ragged RV down a desolate desert road. He's driving like a lunatic. A pair of bodies are sliding back and forth on the RV floor, and a second person in a gas mask, this one a young man, is unconscious in the passenger seat. The masked driver is in a panic and crashes into a ditch.

He staggers out and video records a farewell to his wife and son. Sirens wail in the distance. And then this ordinary looking middle aged man strolls out into the road, a gun in hand, and waits for the sirens.

This is how we are introduced to Walter White (Bryan Cranston) and the world of *Breaking Bad.*

This author maintains that the first season of *Breaking Bad* is very good television that hints at the greatness to come, but is still taking its baby steps. It's highly entertaining. It's a delight to watch. But it is not yet the stuff of television legend.

Which is not a bad thing. Season 1 plays an important role in making the series what it is. It sets the stage for all that comes later, putting in place the puzzle pieces that create the grand tapestry of What Makes Walter White Tick And How He Will Ruin Everything Around Him. We get the core concept behind the show, of course, but also the fine details that make up the world Walt inhabits (and well as glimpses into what truly drives him). So if it doesn't live up to the epic sweep of later seasons, so what? As introductions go, these seven episodes are one of the best.

In the first episode, "Pilot," we learn that the White family is not financially well off, and that Walt's pregnant wife, Skyler (Anna Gunn), is a key force in holding the household together. Their teenage son, Walt. Jr. (RJ Mitte), has cerebral palsy. We also learn that Walt's brother-in-law Hank (Dean Norris) is a Drug Enforcement Agency (DEA) agent, his former student Jesse

Pinkman (Aaron Paul) is a petty criminal who cooks methamphetamine, aka crystal meth, and so on.

The story arc for the first season is relatively straightforward. After receiving a death sentence by way of an inoperable lung cancer diagnoses, Walt decides to cook meth with Jesse – or more accurately, blackmails Jesse into cooking meth with him – ostensibly in order to begin raising money to leave his family after his death. Walt's background in chemistry proves to be a boon, and together they create the best meth New Mexico has ever seen. This grabs the attention of Hank and the DEA. After some hectic ups and downs, including Walt being forced to take two lives, both in self defense, the pair eventually end up in a partnership with a local drug lord.

Walt is on his way to being a legitimate player in the criminal underworld.

The narrative has some memorable ups and downs beginning with the very first episode. The two bodies we glimpse on the floor of the speeding RV are petty drug dealers who intended to rob and kill Walt and Jesse. In desperation, Walt poisons them with an improvised gas, killing one and leaving the other in a stupor. Over the course of a couple of episodes, Walt and Jesse must struggle with how to dispose of one of the bodies – they dissolve it in acid, which hilariously melts away Jesse's bathtub, too, in one of the series' first unforgettable scenes – and with how to deal with the survivor. Walt eventually kills the remaining dealer, but only out of self-defense.

Walt killing the surviving dealer is especially harrowing because he doesn't *want* to kill the guy. He thinks – and continues to think throughout the series – that he can be a criminal without getting his hands dirty. This is just a business that happens to exist outside the law, after all, or so Walt convinces himself. He thinks perhaps he can talk the guy into being civil. Into an understanding. If Walt lets him go he'll just leave and go about his business, no hard feelings, right?

Wrong. Crime doesn't work that way. Our hapless chemistry teacher is forced to choke the dealer to death when he realizes he is going to be killed if he lets him go.

Walter appears to regret having to do this. He's broken up about it. It *hurts* him to have had to kill someone. Even as he goes down the basement stairs knowing the dealer has a shard of broken plate in his possession, knowing he probably plans to kill Walt at the first opportunity, Walt struggles with what he has to do. The signal to the audience is, "This guy isn't really all that bad, he's just a regular guy who made some bad choices." This is a pattern we see throughout the entire series, right until the very end. People lose their lives either by Walter's hand or through his actions and he frets about it, suggests there was no other choice, and moves on.

This early, though, we still buy the lie as readily as Walter and those around him do: Walt is just in over his head. That's all. And we believe it.

Later, the pair enter into an uneasy partnership with a local kingpin named Tuco. Tuco is a stark raving lunatic who kills on a whim. In fact, the pair only get involved with him after he beats Jesse into the hospital, prompting Walt to blow up Tuco's office with improvised explosives (another early classic scene and perhaps the most memorable of the first season).

All of this, however, is merely surface stuff. This is the entertaining part, the exciting narrative that gets things moving forward. The meat of the first season lies beneath the surface.

Take, for instance, Walter's remarkable brilliance. On multiple occasions we are shown that he is no mere high school chemistry teacher. This is a man with a true gift, able to not only synthesize the greatest methamphetamine ever seen in the southwest, but also able to create bombs, poison gas, and more on the fly out of common household goods. More importantly, we learn that he was once a partner in a company called Gray Matter, a pharmaceutical company started by Walt, his old friend Elliot Schwartz, and Gretchen Schwartz, Elliot's wife. Gretchen and Walt were once an item, but Walt, for reasons that are never made explicit but which we can infer, left her in the early days of the company.

Gray Matter, and in turn the Schwartz's, would go on to make many, many millions. Without Walter.

Meanwhile, Walter would go on to teach high school chemistry to bored teenagers, lucky to be making $40,000 a year for the privilege.

This whole corner of Walt's life doesn't play a large role in the *Breaking Bad* narrative, at least not overtly. Elliot finds out about Walt's cancer through Skyler and offers Walt a lucrative job with Gray Matter. Walt, out of pride, declines the offer. Later, when

Walt begins to bring in drug money, he tells Skyler that Elliot and Gretchen agreed to help pay for his cancer treatment. The lie serves as a cover to explain the sudden influx of funds, and (for a time) Skyler suspects nothing.

And that's about it. Gretchen, Elliot, and Gray Matter come and go fairly quickly, their story only a minor subplot in the first two seasons. Aside from a brief reappearance at the show's close, it is forgotten once the narrative really begins to pick up steam.

Yet in truth, it's always there, lingering in the background, because the Walter White that existed prior to the pilot episode is very quietly as important as the Walter White we see on screen. This will be discussed in another chapter in greater detail, but it is essential background material like this that makes paying close attention to the first season so pivotal in grasping the entire sweep of the show and, more importantly, in understanding what makes Walter White tick.

It's important to note that to the writers, nothing we see or know is ever *un*important. Tiny seeds planted in this first season will bloom in the four to come. What we learn about Walt and Jesse here plays a role in every decision they characters make from this point forward. Jesse Pinkman, for instance, seems like little more than a hoodrat druggie when we first meet him, but he eventually develops into the moral center of the show. The roots of that transformation are right here in the first season. Can you spot them? If not, keep reading.

The first season of *Breaking Bad* is many things. It is entertaining. It is often funny. It is well written. It's *damn good television*. So when we say it doesn't rise to the levels of brilliance reached by later seasons, it's not as much an insult as it is a warning to new viewers to keep watching (because it only gets better) and a major *compliment* to later seasons (because holy hell does it ever get better).

This is where the stage is set. Soon, the fun really begins.

Bryan Cranston: The Man Behind the Mask

Bryan Cranston wasn't supposed to be a superstar. Prior to *Breaking Bad*, he had his (cult) moment in the sun as Hal, the father on the Fox sitcom *Malcolm in the Middle*. That had been the pinnacle of his career, and with the show ending as Cranston turned 50 his future prospects for superstardom seemed slim.

He had other roles over the years, of course. Most fans know he was Dr. Tim Whatley, the weirdo dentist on *Seinfeld*. But did you notice him in *Saving Private Ryan*? *The X-Files*? *Hill Street Blues*? *Baywatch*!?

Probably not.

Yet since *Breaking Bad* debuted in 2008, Cranston has won three consecutive Emmy's for Outstanding Lead Actor in a Drama Series (whether he will win his fourth overall is undetermined at the time of this writing) and has become one of the most respected performers in Hollywood. After *Breaking Bad's* finale, Academy Award winning actor Anthony Hopkins even wrote Cranston a letter and told him, "Your performance as Walter White was the best acting I have seen – ever." (1) His ability to instantly fall into character, shimmy between comedy and drama, and generally captivate an audience with mere facial expressions has made him a formidable performer. After years of playing bit parts tinged with comedy, he is now seen as one of the great talents of today.

For what it's worth, though, Cranston thinks talent is only a small part of the puzzle that is his success. You also need to get noticed.

According to Cranston, "It doesn't matter if you're good. If you're just good, you won't succeed. If you have patience and persistence and talent and that's it, you will not have a successful career as an actor. The elusive thing you need is luck." (2)

True enough, and perhaps that realistic view of his place in Hollywood is part of what makes him so endearing to the audience even while his character is doing bad things. He's *genuine*, and that comes across. Off screen, Cranston enjoys a reputation as friendly, humble, and possessing an engaging sense of humor. Indeed, Cranston "has a well-deserved reputation as one of his industry's truly good guys." (3) One might guess that his long struggles to break through may contribute to his humility, but he's far from the first actor to ride to stardom after many years of only minor success, yet one of a few to do so with such affable grace. No, it's probably more accurate to say that he's just a good guy.

Cranston was no stranger to acting growing up. His mother, Audrey Peggy Sell, was a radio actress, and his father, Joseph, was an actor and producer. Neither were particularly successful, though, nor were they stellar parents. "They weren't capable, and we lost the house in a foreclosure. We were kicked out. That's when my brother and I went to live with my grandparents, and my sister and mother lived with my father's mother, which was bizarre. But they had to go someplace." (4) It would be another decade until he saw his father again – perhaps something he drew on to play a father with such an awkward relationship with his son.

In high school he was an athlete, but lacked that "jock-ish" edge. He appeared to be on track for a career in law enforcement when he took an acting class as an elective. The performing bug didn't *completely* bite him, but he dabbled in California theater before getting an acting job at the age of 24 that forced him to move to New York. From there he landed a string of television commercials, voice acting work (including for a number of Japanese anime cartoons under the name Lee Stone), and enough bit parts to keep him gainfully employed. He never became a superstar, but he also never lacked for paying gigs. As the years wore on his breaks got bigger. He landed the role of Buzz Aldrin in HBO's 1998 miniseries *From the Earth to the Moon* and a small part in *Saving Private Ryan* (he played a stateside colonel) before getting his breakthrough role, Hal, the dad on *Malcolm in the Middle*. There he showed himself to be adept at physical comedy, as well as at dancing in his underpants. You might not equate Walter White with comedy, but Cranston's comedic gifts are extensive, and they play a big role in allowing us to sympathize with Walt. His physicality helped make him human.

"He's an immensely physical actor, almost a clown; sometimes a funny clown; other times a very scary clown indeed. The most memorable Walter White moments could almost take place in a silent film," observed GQ magazine. "The man makes a sandwich like Chaplin roller-skated."

Cranston came to Vince Gilligan's attention thanks to a small part he had in a 1998 episode of *The X-Files* called "Drive," which was was penned by Gilligan. In it, Cranston plays an apparently deranged anti-Semite who believes he is suffering from a government-manufactured illness. Cranston's ability to blend humanity and madness, his ability to be both loathsome and sympathetic, left its mark on Gilligan. Years later, when Gilligan came up with the concept of *Breaking Bad*, he had Cranston in mind for the part of Walter White. He would go on to become a key part, if not *the* key part, of the show's puzzle.

> *"We have an amazing ace in hole with Bryan Cranston himself. I knew from Day One that we needed not only an excellent actor – one who can play very dramatic moments and very comedic moments; who has an amazing range as an actor – but also I knew we needed an actor who was human and sympathizable and somehow allowed us to root for him. Who gave us the ability to root for him no matter what he did. And because of Bryan, Walt is always recognizably human, even if he is tremendously flawed as a character." --Vince Gilligan (5)*

Cranston himself never saw Walter as anything but human and relatable, even if only in our darkest daydreams. He believes what happened to Walter White is something we could all succumb to. "My theory is, everyone is capable of being dangerous. We're all capable of inflicting harm to ourselves and to others." (6) Perhaps that's why he was able to portray the character so convincingly. Because he *believes* in him.

A bigger factor may be that Bryan Cranston is just plain easy to like. He's humble. He's funny. He's loved by the people who work with him. Even at the height of his *Breaking Bad* success, he was willing to be the butt of jokes. He conducted staged podcast interviews with Adam Carolla (7) that made him look like a pompous jerk, willing to look bad in order to get laughs. He attended comic conventions. He had countless interactions with fans, almost all of which were positive. And he laughed. A *lot*. This was not a man caught up in his success, this was a man grateful for the chances he had been given. "If you come from an uninspired, aimless youth, with no money and a tremendous amount of misdirection, it's nearly impossible to feel elitist or entitled. Anything that comes to me is a gift." (4)

Hard not to like that.

With the depth to which Cranston dives into Walter White, you might assume that he's a method actor, someone who truly inhabits his character during shooting. Not so. In fact, quite the opposite. Cranston only becomes Walter White after slipping into costume.

> *"When I go to work, I put on the clothes and they help me see the man. I get into his head and I play the man and I stay in the man. Depending on the given scene, sometimes I have to stay in him throughout breaks in order to hold onto a certain thing that might be more difficult than others. But through 31 years of doing this professionally, it's become easier for me to turn it on and turn it off, turn it on and turn it off. That's the way you want it to be. I want the drama to be in the scene and not in the life." --Bryan Cranston (3)*

This isn't to say that he doesn't draw from within himself to bring Walter White to life. You cannot paint a picture as complex as this without tapping into something elemental, something deep in your psyche. For Cranston, it was reaching back to a vision he once had. He was being harassed by an ex-girlfriend, a crazed woman on drugs pounding on his apartment door. When the harassment finally became unbearable, his mind wandered to a dark place.

> *"In my mind, I opened the door—I was living in New York at the time—and I grabbed her by her hair, and I pulled her into my apartment. And on one wall of my apartment is real brick. A brick wall, 12 feet high. And I took her head, and I smashed it against the brick. Over and over and over again. Until I could see—I saw the blood splattering! I saw the brain matter! I saw...I envisioned that I killed her. Because I had that experience, I know it's possible in everyone. I was dangerous at that moment. And the meekest person among us, given the right circumstances, could become dangerous, too." –Bryan Cranston (8)*

It's horrifying to read, but this realization, this moment of reflection, is what informs Walter White. Cranston manages to grab a little honesty from within himself and bring it to life in a way we can relate to even when we're watching him do terrible things. And if we pause to reflect, many of us will realize that we've had those moments, too. Moments when our minds wandered to dark places and conjured up dark deeds. We don't act on them. We don't even necessarily *want* to act on them. But we're aware that this tiny corner of ourselves exists; that it's buried down under layers of what makes us who we are; and that idea is a little frightening.

The willingness to bring that to life with absolutely no fear is not what makes Cranston's portrayal of Walter White so compelling, it's his willingness to do so with an honesty that borders on chilling.

That it comes from such a good man, though, is rather comforting.

1) Uproxx, "Anthony Hopkins Wrote This Fan Letter To Bryan Cranston After Binge-Watching 'Breaking Bad' in Two Weeks," October 14, 2013

2) GQ Magazine, "The Last Stand of Walter White," August 2013

3) HitFix, "Bryan Cranston discusses the 'Breaking Bad' season," June 13, 2010

4) Rolling Stone, "Bryan Cranston on Walter White's Morality," September 13, 2013

5) The Daily Beast, "Breaking Bad Finale: Lost Interviews With Bryan Cranston & Vince Gilligan," September 29, 2013

6) Rolling Stone, "Bryan Cranston Reveals Walter White's Motives," September 17, 2013

7) Adam Carolla, "Adam Carolla and Bryan Cranston Phone Interview," August 7, 2013

8) Newsweek, "TV's Most Dangerous Show," June 26, 2011

THE FATHER-SON RELATIONSHIP FROM HELL

Breaking Bad is a show about many things. Motivations. Choices. Consequences. It is also a show about family. The way we lean on one another, the way we clean up after one another; fractures and forgiveness, sacrifice and selfishness; it runs the gamut from sweet to sinister, pathetic to poignant.

Yet the familial relationship that speaks most strongly to the way in which the bonds we form can also cause us tremendous loss and pain is not a true family relationship. Rather, it is the twisted father/son relationship between Walt and Jesse.

When we first meet him, Walter White is a family man. His relationship with his wife, Skyler, is the sort of on-autopilot marriage we see so much on TV (and too often in real life). He's the sad sack working to bring home a paycheck; she keeps the house running smooth. Their son, Walt. Jr., is a disabled teenager with all the quirks of a typical teenager. Walter appears to love him, but there is a distance there. They don't really have a *relationship*. When we see Walt do things for his son it's often to prove a point or to get one over on Skyler. In the rare instances when he offers advice to his son, it's part of his efforts to cover up his criminal activities.

Their father/son relationship is empty.

Instead, what fatherly instincts Walter White has – and they're not very good instincts – are directed towards his surrogate son, Jesse Pinkman, a former student who did poorly in high school and who fell into dealing drugs after graduation.

Interestingly, this relationship was not supposed to happen, or rather, it wasn't intended to become central to the show. By now the story is famous enough that it doesn't need to be detailed, but it goes like this: Vince Gilligan's original plan was to have Jesse killed at the end of the first season, providing Walt with a stark lesson on the consequences of getting involved in criminal life.

> *"I feel crazy saying this now, but I initially liked the idea of killing off Jesse so that Mr. White would feel very guilty and feel very pained at what he had caused to happen. I figured that that guilt and that pain would lead to some sort of drama, but honestly, I didn't get much*

farther than that. I suppose probably what would have happened is that Jesse would have departed the scene and Walt would have felt the need to partner up with someone else. But my thoughts on this matter were a bit vague, and luckily we did away with the idea very quickly once we cast Aaron Paul. He's such a wonderful young actor that as soon as we saw him on the set, playing against Bryan Cranston and holding his own with an actor that good, I came to realize at that point that it was truly a dumb idea to kill off this great character." –Vince Gilligan (1)

The choice was the right one, because the show may never have become the juggernaut it became without the dynamic interplay between those two characters.

As much as these two attempt to operate as partners in crime, it is clear from the start that Walt is in charge and that Jesse, despite being the one with drug dealing experience, is initially only along for the ride. When we first meet him, Jesse is a dumbass with a mean self-destructive streak, hardly the sort of person you would want your kids to pal around with, but it's difficult not to feel bad for him. Walt emotionally abuses him. He takes his frustrations out on him, demeans him, demoralizes him. He protects him, too, yes, but you get the sense it's not out of altruism. Instead, it's about something Walt has desperately lacked in his life: control. Now able to control something, now actually having someone he can order around, Walter takes full advantage of Jesse's weakness.

Yet at times there is a tenderness here that we don't see between Walter and Walt Jr., a sense that despite his scorn for this inept student, Walt cares for him perhaps even more than he cares for his own son. The few instances of true selflessness we see from Walt – or as close to true selflessness as Walter White can muster – generally center around Jesse. He goes toe-to-toe with a brilliant drug lord (Gus Fring) over Jesse. He kills two street level drug dealers in order to save the young man's life, Walt's first act of cold-blooded murder. Even in Walt's final moments, after initially intending to kill Jesse, he makes a last-second decision to spare him from the assault of gunfire Walt is about to unleash on a group of neo-Nazis who stole his money.

Walt never puts himself further out for someone than he does for Jesse.

Perhaps he sees something of himself in the young man, something Walt Jr. just doesn't (or can't) have. Maybe Walt realizes that he could have been like Jesse if he made bad choices as a young man, or maybe he realizes that Jesse isn't the shallow kid he first believed him to be. Exactly what he sees is never quite clear, but what *is* clear is that something in this young man stirs a protectiveness in Walt that at times even manages to do battle with his inner Heisenberg.

None of these are entirely pure moments, of course. Walter needed Jesse both as a partner and because he needed someone he could manipulate and control. Someone like Gale Boetticher (David Costabile) just wouldn't do; Gale was too smart, too capable, too able to live his own life. He was already a fully formed adult. Jesse was a lump of clay. Walt could mold him and shape him – not for Jesse's benefit, but for Walt's. Even Walter's battles with Gus over Jesse were not entirely altruistic. This sparring was as much about Walter's unconscious need to fight with authority as it was about considering what was best for Jesse. If Gus would not let Jesse be Walt's cook partner then dammit, Jesse would become the *only* person who would work in the role, even if only so Walt could assert some kind of feeble dominance over Gus.

Tragically for Jesse, he needs to be controlled by someone, too – or at least a part of him allows it to happen. Estranged from his parents, out on his own without anyone who truly cares for him, the only people Jesse has in his life other than Walter White are a trio of drug-addled losers who offer him plenty of laughs but little else. His parents have given up on him. They love him, but they can't cope with his drug use and poor habits, especially not when they have a model son at home to take pride in. So all Jesse has are friends who are also caught up in the drug world. As viewers we love Badger, Skinny Pete and (to a lesser extent) Combo, but it's clear they are no good for him.

Mr. White, however, seems to push Jesse to do better. To improve. To reach his true potential. This support is partially a farce, of course – Walt taking Jesse under his wing is to a large extent self-serving – but it provides Jesse with a foundation he did not previously have. He's never before had someone urge him to be his best, so even if it comes in the form of an abusive relationship, Jesse can't help but embrace it. He *needs* it. This is not atypical for those in abusive relationships, which Walt and Jesse's certainly is.

"They don't stay for the pain. Their desperate, often palpable hope, if you sit in the room with them, is that the abuse will go away. And they tend to block out all evidence to the contrary. In point of fact, they stay for love. Many abuse survivors cling to the *positive* traits in their partners – like being affectionate and reliable." (2) Despite his negative influence, Walt also provides Jesse with some of the only positive reinforcement he has in his life – so he stays.

As we come to discover over the course of the show, Jesse wasn't really the ratty, untrustworthy loser we first meet. Not in his heart. "I felt like he was trying to be something that he really wasn't. I knew that in the beginning," Aaron Paul (3) said of his view of the real Jesse Pinkman, and he's right. What Jesse really wanted from his life can be glimpsed in the brief flashback (or daydream sequence; it's unclear which it is) in the series finale, "Felina." In this sequence, he is working on the one good thing he ever accomplished in his life – a wooden box he carved in high school and eventually traded away for drugs. Jesse was a good person, perhaps the purest adult on the show, who happened to fall in with the wrong crowd at an early age and never bounced back from it. He was young and irresponsible, yes, but he still had a vast future in which to discover why he was put on the Earth. For a brief moment in his life, Mr. White may have been the man who could help him discover that.

The exact opposite happens. Mr. White dismantles everything Jesse holds dear and leaves him an empty shell. Walt adopted a son and promptly remade him in his own image: numb, barren, dissatisfied, and only able to clutch at small victories bereft of morality. It's not his goal, not consciously, but it is the natural result of being adopted by Walter White.

Whether this is because Walt is incapable of being a good father is an open question. We certainly get few answers when we look at his relationship with his *real* son. Whatever Walter's relationship with his actual son is, we get the sense that Walt doesn't consider him as capable of much more than being the kid who eats a lot of breakfast. He doesn't confide in him. He is not truthful with him. And he expects nothing from him.

Jesse, on the other hand, opens up something inside Walt that allows some genuine goodness to seep through. Up until the finale, during which Walt finally tells Skyler the truth about what motivated him, Jesse is one of the only people who got an entirely truthful statement from Walt, and in a depraved way it resonates as one of the show's most tender. In "One Minute," a third season episode that is one of the series' best, Jesse lies in a hospital bed, beaten and bruised after being attacked by Hank. There, Jesse finally finds the strength to reject Walt. Tells him he ruined his life. For a moment Walter seems to recognize what he did to this young man, how he ran him down and crushed any scrap of self worth he had, and he offers what is to Walt one of the warmest statements he can muster: "Your meth is good, Jesse. As good as mine."

This is the prism through which Walter now sees things. It is the prism through which he judges Jesse, and it is the measure of their father/son relationship.

That, alas, is their twisted reality.

At the very end, when Jesse leaves Walter to die alone in a meth lab and Jesse himself flees across the desert, screaming with a primal mix of joy and relief, he is escaping more than captivity. He is escaping the oppressive household in which he had lived for the last two years: The House of Mr. White, his dark father.

1) AMC Blog, "Breaking Bad Series Creator Answers Viewers Questions, Part III," October 11, 2011

2) Psychology Today, "Why Do People Stay In Abusive Relationships?," March 6, 2013

3) HitFix, "Breaking Bad star Aaron Paul looks back at Jesse Pinkman's Greatest Hits," July 11, 2012

BREAKING DOWN SEASON 2

Walter White is a smart man. He is a brilliant man. You would think he would learn quickly that the world he has stepped into is not one made for pasty middle-aged men, especially after meeting with Tuco Salamanca turns into a near walk into an early grave.

When it comes to criminals, Tuco is everything Walt thinks he is not. Tuco is wild and crazed, loves to dabble in the drugs he sells, and enjoys hurting people for no other reason than the thrill of it. Even at this early stage, Walt fancies himself a businessman making rational, albeit illegal, decisions in order to earn his living. He is none of these things, of course – few things Walter White does once he decides to cook meth are truly rational – but he believes he can operate in the criminal world and still retain a semblance of morality.

Season 2 is about Walter White coming to find how terribly wrong he is about that, and more importantly, about his choice to turn down a dark path once and for all.

After Tuco's death and a brief period during which both Walt and Jesse begin to rebuild all that had fallen apart around them – Jesse finds himself a new place to live and a girlfriend, and Walt begins to construct the grand lies he'll use to keep his family away from the truth – the pair again begin to cook meth. Walt pitches the idea as a necessity; he needs the money to pay for his mounting cancer treatments. What Walt doesn't tell Jesse is that he had an opportunity to have those bills paid via Elliot and Gretchen Schwartz, his former partners in a now successful pharmaceutical company called Gray Matter. But pride wouldn't let him accept a job or money. The Gray Matter days still gnaw at him. Walt left the company under somewhat unclear circumstances – he had a falling out with Gretchen, who was his girlfriend at the time, but the nature of the falling out is never specified – and Elliot and Gretchen went on to become successful, respected, and wealthy.

(Incidentally, this background material is absolutely vital to understanding the character of Walter White, yet creator Vince Gilligan and his team wisely chose to *keep* it in the background. This story, after all, is about where Walter is now, not where he *has* been.)

So despite having nearly been killed by the lunacy of Tuco, Walt talks Jesse into cooking meth again. This time they recruit a few of Jesse's offbeat friends (Badger, Skinny Pete and Combo) to help sell the meth they produce.

And naturally, it goes bad for them pretty quickly. Skinny Pete is robbed at knifepoint by two meth-heads, and Walt is furious about it. Steal from Walter, the great Heisenberg? He'll not tolerate that, so he does what has become so easy for him (and will continue to be easy for him): he manipulates Jesse into acting in a way contrary to Jesse's nature.

What is striking about how events then play out is how willingly Walt will embrace evil deeds even this early in his evolution, yet how quickly he will balk when he realizes just what he is doing. Where he shines when this happens is in recovering from his botched decisions and turning them to his advantage.

For instance, when Skinny Pete is robbed, Walt gives Jesse a gun and tells him to "take care of it." The implication is clear. He wants Jesse to go do murder for him. That's not merely cold, it's outright *evil.*

But a couple days later he realizes what he asked of Jesse and tells him not to do it. Change of heart. He can't ask something that dire of him.

Too late. Jesse already went to the house and the meth-head Walt wanted him to kill is already dead –not at Jesse's hands, but at the hands of the addict's "skank" wife. Word on the street is that Jesse did the murder, though, despite the truth being much different. And this is where Walt shows himself adept at adaptation. Rather than being relieved that he didn't push Jesse into something evil, Walt sees the turn of events as an opportunity. He embraces the rumors. Encourages them. In doing this, he gets to feel as if he didn't manipulate Jesse into doing something horrible, thus allowing him to continue thinking he's treading a moral path, even while using rumors of Jesse's "murder" to add menace to the Heisenberg name.

This is the Gray Matter baggage rising to the surface. Walt feels powerless and used in his life, so in turn he uses others, giving himself a sense of power he could never enjoy previously.

This becomes clear in one of the best conversations of the series, and one all fans remember well: Walt and Gretchen chatting at the restaurant. Gretchen offering sympathy for what Walt has become. Walt telling her, "Fuck you." His resentment is immense. His jealously, his sense of being used, all of it is weighty and palpable. It's breathtaking stuff.

Walter's resentment is not contained to his former partners at Gray Matter, either, nor even to the ordinary life he is driven to escape from. As Jesse begins to develop a relationship with his neighbor, Jane Margolis (Krysten Ritter), Walt grows uneasy with the arrangement. Some of it is justified. Prompted first by a traumatic experience during which he cares for a child neglected by meth-head parents (See "Jesse Pinkman, Our Unlikely Moral Conscience"), and then further triggered by the murder of his friend Combo, who had been selling meth on Jesse and Walt's behalf, Jesse falls back into drug addiction. Jane is a recovering addict, and before long the two of them are using together. Jesse even begins using something he had never dabbled in before, heroin. Walt is disgusted by this. He never really respected Jesse, but now he can't trust him, either. The situation grows so bad that Jesse almost blows a deal worth over $1 million after passing out in a drug-induced stupor.

But Walt also resents the situation because Jane is asserting more control over Jesse than he is. His partner is no longer at his beck and call. He is no longer so easy to manipulate. And this, well, this burns at Walt. After all, his real reasons for getting involved in the drug business were control, pride and ego. Losing his grasp on Jesse to some young junkie is too much to bear.

And this is where Walt's pride once again steers him wrong (as it will many times). He executes a major deal with a regional fast food chain owner, Gus Fring (Giancarlo Esposito), and in the process nets himself and Jesse more money than they've ever seen in their life. Walt then takes it upon himself to hold Jesse's money for him. Jesse is just a junkie, he insists, and until he gets clean, Walt will serve as caretaker for his share of the proceeds.

It's a step over the line, and even the drug-addled Jane can see that. She grabs the reins, takes control of the situation, and promptly blackmails Walt. Either turn over Jesse's money to him, she tells him, or she'll blow the lid on what Walt has been involved in.

Walt gives in. What else could he do? Now these two junkies have more money than they ever imagined. With money in hand, Jesse and Jane dream of running away and living a life together, free of all the bullshit they deal with in Albuquerque. But first, one last night of drugs before they leave.

This is where Walter truly breaks bad once and for all.

Walt enters Jesse's apartment late at night to find Jesse and Jane passed out. Both had been shooting up heroin and are in a stupor. Walt attempts to wake Jesse and in the process accidentally knocks Jane onto her back. She vomits and begins to choke in her sleep.

Walter watches.

That's all. He just watches.

Part of this show's beauty, and part of the genius of the writers, is that they know when to shut up. That's what happens here. They let Bryan Cranston's face do all the heavy lifting. The man says *so much* without saying a word. Jane is choking to death; she is going to die. No one knows but him, and he can save her. With almost no effort he can save her life. Instead he watches. He's horrified and sickened by what he sees, but you also see the wheels turning in his head. He knows that if she dies the danger of her ratting him out dies with her. He's briefly tormented by this, by what he is allowing to happen, by *himself*, but he lets her die all the same.

And that all comes across despite him not having a single line of dialogue.

In many ways, it's Walter White's last moment as a human being.

"That decision was his turning point and there was no going back," (1) Ritter told Vulture. The scene was a difficult one for Cranston. "In one take, I saw my own daughter dying in front of me, and that choked me up. That's the worst thing for a parent." (2)

Season 2 ends with one of the show's most absurd events – but in a show that had an absurdist leaning from the first episode, it doesn't feel entirely out of place. Donald Margolis (John de Lancie), Jane's father, had looked after Jane with perhaps the deepest love we see from a father in this show. Concerned about her addiction and intent on helping her work through it, the news that she overdosed shatters every part of his being. He lives in a daze for a few weeks before returning to his job as an air traffic controller.

There, still distracted, still distraught, he inadvertently allows two aircraft to collide over Albuquerque. In the crash, 167 people die.

Fittingly, debris from the crash splashes down in Walter's pool. A pink teddy bear, singed, an eye torn out. It's a call forward to the eventual fate of Gus Fring, but more importantly it's symbolic of the shattered innocence Walt leaves in his wake. Those people on the flight of Wayfarer 515 did not die by Walter's hand, but the far-ranging consequences of his decision to let Jane die certainly nudged their lives in a new (and tragic) direction. This happens time and again. Walt acts, and the people around him suffer. If Walt understands this, he doesn't do so consciously. After all, the person he is most adept at lying to is himself. He convinces himself that Combo's death, Jane's death, the plane crash, these things are not on him. He *must* convince himself of this, because he can't allow himself to recognize that he has reached the point of no return. The crash is symbolic of this. Walt's worlds have collided, his family is fracturing, people are dying, and there is no way to put the pieces back together again.

If the first season was about setting the stage for Walter's transformation and giving us the tools we need to understand what truly drives him, the second season is about Walt making the final decision to truly break bad. This is about his choice to be a villain, even if he doesn't acknowledge it at the time. He could have left the business after things went bad with Tuco. He could have found another means to pay for his treatment. He could have been truthful with his family. He could have saved that young woman's life.

Instead, he chose Heisenberg.

1) Vulture, "Krysten Ritter Breaking Bad: Team Walter Until The Bitter End," September 24, 2013

2) HitFix, "Breaking Bad star Bryan Cranston looks back on Walter White's greatest hits, part 1," July 12, 2012

The Law of Unintended Consequences or *New Mexico Has Cancer*

New Mexico has cancer. And that cancer's name is Walter White.

I can't claim credit for the observation. That belongs to a fellow *Breaking Bad* fan who shared it with me during a conversation about the way in which Walt impacts those around him. When exploring the law of unintended consequences – a core theme of this show – it's hard to argue with the notion that cancer victim Walter White is himself a cancer.

The obvious observation, of course, is the simple one: he creates an especially potent version of a particularly insidious drug. Through his work, countless thousands in his community and beyond fall into desperate, loathsome lives of addiction and crime. That alone makes him a blight on the world around him.

Yet it's more than that. After all, Walter White did not invent methamphetamine. It was in his community before he came onto the scene. From small-time slingers like Jesse Pinkman to major crime lords like Gustavo Fring, meth had already been rotting lives away. No, the cancer that is Walter White is more indirect, but in many ways even more destructive.

Chalk it up to the Law of Unintended Consequences.

First explored by philosopher Adam Smith, most famous for his work *The Wealth of Nations*, and defined and popularized in the Twentieth Century by sociologist Robert K. Merton in his 1936 essay "The Unanticipated Consequences of Social Action," the Law says that your actions have outcomes that are not expected, and outcomes that may be contrary to the purpose of your actions in the first place.

In modern fiction, Walter White and the maelstrom that surrounds his post-cancer life is one of the great examples of the law of unintended consequences in action.

Walt, of course, believes he is only doing minor evil in order to accomplish a greater good. As argued elsewhere, this is a lie he tells himself, but for the purposes of this discussion let's take his lie at face value: Walt just wants to provide for his family, protect what he's doing, and protect his young apprentice, Jesse.

Noble enough on the surface, until you begin to see just what that means for those around him.

Person after person, many whom Walt doesn't even know and will never meet, have their lives upended either directly or indirectly due to Walt's actions. The list is stunningly long once you begin to break it down. (In September 2013, *The Daily Caller* published a great visual list of all those deaths). (1)

Take, for instance, Jane, her father, and by proxy the many hundreds impacted by the plane crash caused by Jane's father. No, Walter is not directly responsible for either Jane's death (though he could have prevented it) or the crash of Wayfarer 515, but each event is the fallout of choices Walt made.

Other than Jane herself, Jesse appears most to blame for her overdose, but take a closer look at how the pair got to the overdose moment. Jesse had cleaned himself up when Walt pressured him to go murder two junkies who had robbed Skinny Pete. Jesse didn't end up doing it, but had a traumatizing experience instead, one that scarred him for the rest of the series. Later, Jesse's friend Combo is murdered, a murder that would not have taken place had Walt not pushed Jesse into overseeing distribution of the meth they cook. Seeing the horror of the meth household – the squalid living conditions, the horrible parents, and the terrible future that awaited a little boy he briefly grew to care about – and experiencing the senseless murder of a friend sent Jesse over the edge and back into drugs. Walt's utter disregard for the young man's mental well-being was the primary factor in his descent back into drugs.

In turn, Jesse getting back into drugs exposed Jane to it. She resisted at first, but through weakness, her addiction, and her affection for Jesse, she caved. Finally, Walt's ego tripping decision to play games with Jesse's cash, something he had no right to do, prompted Jesse and Jane to have one last reckless night before skipping town.

This is a terrible loss for Donald Margolis, Jane's father, an air traffic controller who returns to work while still mourning the death of the young daughter he cared for so much. He's distracted at work, and his inattention leads to two planes colliding over

Albuquerque, killing 167 people in all and causing extensive property damage.

Jesse and Jane are responsible for their own actions, as is Mr. Margolis, but without Walt's involvement, without his actions, their fate is different. By proxy he is culpable in these events. He's not *solely* at fault, but he played a role in causing these tragic events to unfold. This is the law of unintended consequences at work, and it is something we see throughout the show.

And then we have Hank and Marie, one of whom was killed directly due to Walt's actions and the other who was left a broken widow. This one is especially tragic because Hank was one of the show's only good guys. Yes, he was a brash, often offensive caricature of machismo, but he was also one of the few who wanted to stop crime rather than engage in it. He didn't need to die. Walt could have turned himself in. Instead, Walt chose to try and outmaneuver him. The end result for Hank could only be bad. Walt knew this, but he did it anyway.

Or Bogdan Wolynetz (Marius Stan), Walt's former boss at his part-time car wash job. The guy was a jerk, but he also appeared to be an honest man who had a business to run. Being a jerk doesn't mean you deserve to have your livelihood taken from you through dishonesty, but Walter's never-ending need to pull more people into his growing storm mean Bogdan was fated to contract the same cancer eating away at everyone else who came in contact with Walt.

Ted Beneke is another unsympathetic-but-innocent character whose life is upended thanks to the law of unintended consequences. Ted slept with Skyler, yes, but he certainly wasn't alone in what he did – she is culpable there, too – and it doesn't mean he deserved to be nearly paralyzed for it. Skyler entered into the affair willingly, and she did so as a reaction to Walt's continued lies and deception. If Walt isn't a chronic liar deceiving the people he claims to love, Skyler never turns to Ted for comfort. And if Walt isn't revealed to be cooking meth, she never takes it a step further and enters into an extended affair – which itself was in large part a ploy by Skyler to force Walt out of the house in order to get him away from the children.

Ted's life was already heading towards trouble, but when the Whites came into the picture, things went from bad to worse for him.

And then there are the unsympathetic bad guys who get tangled in Walt's wires. Saul Goodman, Gustavo Fring, Mike Ehrmantraut, Gus's loyal henchman Victor, Combo, and many others see things go bad for them – often because they are *killed* – thanks in no small part to becoming involved with Walter White. He was the X factor that steered them well off course and ruined all they had. Sure, they were unsavory characters and would have been involved in unseemly things one way or another – you're not supposed to feel *sorry* for them – but that's not really the point. The point is that whenever Walt enters the picture, bad things happen.

This is the law of unintended consequences at work. These people had their lives shattered by him, either directly or indirectly. The show seems to tell us that evil deeds are magnified, and doing bad things for a good end doesn't work because you're inevitably going to pull everyone around you under, too. That some of these people were already bad doesn't really matter. What matters is that by being pulled into Walt's orbit, they had their lives ruined. This is a central theme upon which *Breaking Bad* is built.

While those most directly impacted by Walt's actions are bad people, or at the very least morally ambiguous – even Skyler is compromised by the end – often it ends up being total innocents caught in the crossfire. The flight of Wayfarer 515 is an indirect example of innocents harmed due to the cancer that is Walter White. A more direct example are the bodies left in the wake of Leonel and Marco Salamanca, the fearsome Cartel cousins of crazed drug lord Tuco.

If the cousins committed murder – their body count numbers over a dozen just during their hunt for "Heisenberg" –can we blame Walt for that? We can. They were specifically on an obsessed mission to kill Walt, and were doing so to avenge Tuco, who would still be alive had he not gotten involved with Heisenberg. If they're not out to take down this mysterious drug manufacturer, all those innocents in their way never get killed. A truck full of immigrants. A handicapped woman whose van they steal. An old woman and tribal police officer they kill on a reservation. The fact that they didn't die by Walter's hand doesn't matter; they still died *because* of him.

Walt doesn't *intend* for all those innocents to die, of course, but intentions are irrelevant. The things he did prompted the Cousins to seek revenge. Innocents died because of it. Those are the unintended consequences of his actions, and it's a key example of the insidious cancer that is Walter White.

The greatest example of the law of unintended consequences at work, and the one that has been central to the show from the very first episode, is the deterioration of Jesse Pinkman. Jesse was a typical young slacker before he got involved with Walt. Not a model citizen by any means, but far from a hardened criminal who was going to leave corpses in his wake. He had a rough time with parents who gave up on him; hung out with bad but relatively harmless people; and got caught up in petty crime. Like many other twenty-somethings he was a dope, except he slung a small amount of meth on the side. Not a good guy, to be sure, but hardly evil.

And unlike many of the others around him, Jesse has a conscience. He actually cares about the idea that his actions might hurt people. It pains him in a way it does not pain many of those he comes into contact with. He has a line he will not cross unless forced, a code that he doesn't even think about – it's just naturally ingrained in him – and unlike Walt that line isn't based on selfishness and self-interest, it's based on empathy.

Yet through manipulation, through coercion, through bullying, Walt turns him into a murderer and strips away everything good in his life. No one sums this up better than Jesse himself during one of the show's greatest monologues, his hospital speech from "One Minute" (season 3, episode 7):

> *"Ever since I met you, everything I ever cared about is gone! Ruined, turned to shit, dead! Ever since I hooked up with the great Heisenberg, I have never been more alone! I have nothing! No one! Alright, it's all gone, get it? No, no, no, why … why would you get it? What do you even care, as long as you get what you want, right? You don't give a shit about me! You said I was no good. I'm nothing! Why would you want me, huh?"*

Jesse goes from a carefree petty criminal to a withered, battered young man who sees nothing but ill in the world. He finds love, and then love chokes to death on its own vomit while Walt watches. He finds a surrogate family to care about in Andrea and Brock Cantillo, and it is both poisoned by his partner and takes a bullet to the head from a neo Nazi. He watches children die, friends die, his world crumble. Everything he gets is stripped away.

Jesse is dying of the cancer that is Walter White.

Throughout the course of *Breaking Bad*, Walt insists that he is looking out for Jesse. At times that even appears genuine, too, such as when he runs down the two drug dealers Jesse is about to confront.

But our actions have consequences we don't intend. The choices you make have ripples far beyond your control, and seemingly small actions can have a much larger impact than you intend. It's a lesson Jesse learns the hardest way possible, and one that Walt never seems to learn at all.

1) The Daily Caller, "The complete list of all the deaths Walter White is responsible for," September 26, 2013

THE SHOW'S TEN GREATEST LINES

For all the praise it gets as one of television's greatest dramas, *Breaking Bad* is not a very talky show. As this book is published, the show has never won an Emmy for writing. Many of its most powerful, dramatic moments and deepest looks into its characters come in moments of silence. Actions, facial expressions, subtle body language. All are more powerful in the world of *Breaking Bad* than mere words.

But that's not to say that it hasn't had some fantastic dialogue, because it certainly has. Here are ten of the most memorable lines ever uttered on the show and why they are noteworthy.

"No more half measures, Walter."

When Mike Ehrmantraut gives Walter a lengthy glimpse into his past as a police officer, the story he tells is a harrowing one concerning domestic violence and the way in which our choice to act or not act can have consequences we do not intend. Mike's decision not to kill a serial abuser when he had the chance seemed the moral one when he made it, but two weeks later that decision led to the death of an innocent woman. Mike never really recovered, and the incident probably had a lot to do with his turn towards the wrong side of the law. It's a powerful look into his past, but more importantly it's also a painful bit of irony for Mike, who in making this speech inadvertently encouraged Walt to push forward with his plans to kill Gus.

"Yeah, science!"

Jesse Pinkman's blend of crude street talk and endearing (if rough around the edges) innocence is perhaps most typified in his cry of "Yeah, science!" from the final episode of the first season.

Mr. White has figured out a way to synthesize meth without using over-the-counter drugs, which are typically used by low level meth cooks, and the idea thrills Jesse. Up until then he had no idea that smarts could come in handy. It's both a revelation for him and the start of an evolution, since by the final season Jesse himself would come up with brilliant plans of his own, as well as a look into the almost charming naivety that makes Jesse a fan favorite.

"Run."

One word. Three letters. And more powerful than some of the grandest, most eloquent, most passionately delivered speeches in television history. In an effort to save Jesse's life, Walter had just run over two drug dealers and shot one in the head. It is his first true act of cold-blooded murder, and also one of his few (largely) selfless acts of the series. Even more important, it squares Walter off with the region's crime lord once and for all. Walter White vs. Gustavo Fring has truly begun. But all the audience can think after seeing a shaken Walt step out of his car and command Jesse to flee is, "Holy shit!"

"Say my name."

There are many moments when we see just how prideful and arrogant Walter White can be, but the most pithy – not to mention the most ballsy – is when he stares down the head of another criminal operation, tells them he is the man who killed Gus Fring, and then tries to bully them into a partnership. He knows they realize he is Heisenberg, but that's not good enough. Having recently come out on top in his clash with Gus, he can't help but push things a little further. And so he demands of them, "Say my name." And they do.

"I am the one who knocks."

Walter White is perhaps less frightening than he thinks he is; his reputation as Heisenberg is a brilliant bit of PR, but anyone who knows him knows he does not quite live up to his reputation as a savage criminal drug lord. He is also less secure in himself than he is willing to let on. One of the few places where he can pretend to be larger than he is, is at home. When Skyler is frightened that Walt has placed the family in jeopardy and confronts him about the danger they are in (and they *are* in danger), Walt lets his inner Heisenberg out and directs it toward his wife. In an effort not only to intimidate and convince her that he has things under control, but also to convince *himself*, Walt utters one of the series' classic lines. The question is whether he actually believes his bravado.

"I fucked Ted."

Skyler White wasn't exactly at the high point of her life. Her cancer-stricken husband had been acting erratically and was living a secret second life. To her horror, she discovered that second life was as a methamphetamine manufacturer. This was simply too much to bear, especially with two children in the house. She couldn't force Walt to leave – he simply refused to – so she does something she hopes will drive him from the house and away from the family: she sleeps with her boss and then tells Walt about it in the bluntest terms possible. Anna Gunn's delivery of this powerful line is one of the show's great hammer blows.

"Shut the fuck up and let me die in peace."

Mike Ehrmantraut was *Breaking Bad's* anti-Walter White, a once good man who got on the wrong side of the law but who *realized* he was on the wrong side of the law. He acknowledged his own moral failings and yet still tried to live honorably within the ugly world he had created for himself. Crossing paths with Heisenberg, however, would be his worst mistake. Mike dies at the hands of Walt, who begins to stumble over a rough half-apology while the ex-cop bleeds out before him. Mike never had any respect for Walt, though, and is not inclined to hear Walt's bullshit in his final moments, and tells him as much in no uncertain terms. Right until the end, he was the show's most no-nonsense badass.

"Better call Saul!"

Breaking Bad began as a (very) black comedy, but as time wore on things grew more serious for Walt and Jesse. The supporting cast, led by Saul Goodman (Bob Odenkirk), stepped up to bring much needed levity to the proceedings. Saul's offbeat sense of humor, rapid-fire delivery and completely absent sense of morality made him a fan favorite from the moment he came onto the scene. He became such a favorite, in fact, that the character is set to get a spinoff series of his own. Saul himself is best typified in the slimy slogan gracing his ultra-slimy ads, three simple words that tell us that this guy is a dirtbag – and we love him for it.

"If that's true, if you really don't know who I am, then maybe your best course would be to tread lightly."

Hank has finally figured out the Heisenberg puzzle. Turns out the mysterious meth cook had been under his nose all along. It's his brother-in-law, Walt. He could succumb to feelings of betrayal, but instead he gets to work figuring out how to bring Walt down. Trouble is, Walter is at the height of his arrogance at this point, so without coming right out and saying that Hank is right about him, he instead denies being Heisenberg ... just before dishing out a chilling threat. It was a hold-your-breath moment in one of the tensest episodes of the series.

"Just because you shot Jesse James doesn't make you Jesse James."

Yes, we're back to Mike again. He rarely had much to say, so when he *did* say something you had damned well better listen. Walter is basking in the glory of having killed Gus Fring. He thinks he's ready to take over the vast crime empire over which Gus ruled. Mike, however, knows better. Perceptive and astute, he sees that Walt is full of himself. He also sees that Walt is about to bite off more than he can chew, recognizing that no good can come of this ex-teacher indulging in fantasies of ruling the roost. Mike is right about that, too ... but in the end being right doesn't save his life.

BREAKING DOWN SEASON 3

When Walter White turns the corner and breaks bad for good in season 2, it can only mean that his life is about to get a lot more complicated. Things are going to fall apart around him, those close to him will begin to face the consequences of his actions, and all that he thinks he's working towards will turn to ash in his mouth.

That is the core theme of season 3. The decay. The collapse. The realization that the control Walter sought to have over his life is impossible to grasp. And the horrifying realization that in order to keep moving forward, he's going to have to corrupt others, too.

The season opens with a disturbing scene. We're deep in the Mexican desert. Men and women are on their bellies, crawling across the dirt. The air is ominous. A hazy orange hue tints everything. A car arrives on the scene, and two bald, impeccably dressed young men step out, look around, and they, too, get on their bellies and begin to crawl. The group reach a one-room adobe hut. The pair of well-dressed men get up and go inside. There they find a drawing of someone we know: Heisenberg.

They are hunting for Walter White.

Back in New Mexico, Walt is already dealing with the fallout of his actions. The city is in mourning over the crash of Wayfarer 515. His continued lies have prompted Skyler to move out with the children in order to give Walt time to pack his things and get out. His partner in crime, Jesse, is a lost soul sleepwalking his way through rehab. In effect, what little Walt has is in the process of escaping from his grasp. This is accelerated when he reveals the truth to Skyler: the money that has paid for his treatments and kept a roof over their head is drug money.

But wait, he insists, it's all over now. He's leaving the meth cooking business. He only did it for the family, anyway, and now he's done. That's good enough, right? Of course not. Skyler will not have her children in the same house with a man who manufactures drugs for a living, and who can blame her?

As Walt's family situation disintegrates, he briefly resists getting involved with the business again, thinking perhaps he can salvage things, but Gustavo Fring, the business-like drug lord who runs Mexican Cartel business in New Mexico, continues to try and recruit Walt as his new cook. The blue meth is proving very profitable. If Walter can continue to provide it, it would be lucrative for both of them. Walt refuses for a while, but the lure soon proves impossible to resist.

What Walt doesn't realize is that he and his family are about to face the unintended consequences of Tuco's death early in season 2. In fact, *everyone* is about to experience the unintended consequences of the decisions Walter and Jesse made not just in season 2, but starting from the very first episode.

The entire season plays out as a series of decisions that go bad for Walt and Jesse. Walter's lies push Skyler into Ted Beneke's bed. Skyler's infidelity strengthens Walter's resolve to hold the family together, even if only so he can say he *won.* Sloppy work allows Hank to get within a single aluminum RV wall of catching Walt and Jesse. Jesse is beaten into the hospital by Hank, and in perhaps the most moving, revelatory scene of the series, comes to realize that Walter is merely manipulating him. Jesse's instinctually protective attitude towards children first puts him in a kill or be killed position, and then threatens to topple not only the arrangement with Gus, but to put both he and Walt into an early grave. And Walt's tug-of-war with Gus ends up with him pushing Jesse into his darkest deed yet, cold-blooded murder.

The latter twist is where not just the season, but the entire series finally takes a left turn into the land of Never-Ending Tension.

But first, let's rewind to when Jesse almost got himself and Walter caught. Walt's brother-in-law, DEA agent Hank Schrader, isn't quite the wise-cracking dumbass we met in the early episodes. As we come to learn, his gutter humor and bravado are largely a mask for someone who doesn't like to let his guard down. Hank doesn't like to show his emotions, doesn't like to show weakness, and doesn't like to acknowledge sincerity. He's an alpha largely because he knows no other way to protect himself. That's why we're surprised at just how insightful and intuitive he can be in his hunt for Heisenberg. Following a series of clues, he manages to identify the famous *Breaking Bad* RV and track it to a junkyard … just as Walter and Jesse are about to have it destroyed. Only some quick thinking by Walt allows him and Jesse to escape, but he pulls it off with a dirty trick. Walt stages a call to Hank's cell phone saying his wife, Marie (Betsy Brandt), had been in a horrific accident, which pulls him off the scene before he can catch the meth-cooking pair.

Walt's trick has dire consequences for Jesse. Hank assumes Jesse somehow tricked him. The idea that the kid used Marie in his ploy – that he even knows her name and his personal cell phone number – infuriates Hank, so he storms into Jesse's house and beats him so bad he ends up in the hospital. The beating is so severe that Hank is on the verge of losing his badge.

Walter, of course, doesn't really care about any of this provided he escapes capture and continues to indulge in being Heisenberg. Gus offers him huge amounts of cash to cook meth for him, but Walt is still playing games, still trying to get Jesse aboard. And from a hospital bed Jesse finally sees Walt for what he is. We've referenced this before, but it's worth revisiting:

> *"Ever since I met you, everything I ever cared about is gone! Ruined, turned to shit, dead! Ever since I hooked up with the great Heisenberg I have never been more alone! I HAVE NOTHING!"*

This comes in the midst of one of the five best episodes of the series, "One Minute," which has some of the most emotionally trying scenes as well as some of its most thrilling. Aaron Paul earned an Emmy almost entirely for this episode and for this scene.

And then the episode explodes into violence when the Cousins come shooting for Hank. All hell breaks loose, and the foolish notion Walt had that he could insulate his family from what he was doing is shattered by bullets and blood.

Considering how far things have fallen already, it's almost astonishing that at this point the season is still only half over. But sure enough, there is plenty of time for things to get worse – and things do indeed get worse. Walt and Jesse begin to cook again like "normal," this time cooking for Gus Fring, but while in rehab Jesse meets Andrea Cantillo (Emily Rios), a former addict with a young son. He also discovers that Andrea's younger brother, Tomas (Angelo Martinez), is the one who shot and killed his friend Combo. The double revelation of finding out who killed his friend as well as the fact that it was a child who did the shooting sends Jesse over the edge. He's got to confront the man who allowed this to happen, Gus, and make him understand you can't operate this way. It's a bold move, a selfless move, and not too long ago one we wouldn't have expected from Jesse. But this is a young man going through a spiritual awakening. Pushed and pulled by Mr. White, he's increasingly directed by his moral code rather than the terse demands of his partner in crime. It's a trait that doesn't always serve his interests, but as we come to discover, Jesse's own interests are not his priority.

The final two episodes of this season are among the most potent of the series and boast some of its most gripping moments. Jesse is on the verge of killing two drug dealers against Gus's orders (and giving himself a death sentence in the process) when Walter intervenes, running the dealers down and then shooting one in the head. It is his first act of true murder. He leaves Jesse with one word: "Run." Cut to credits.

Even now you can still feel the audience holding its breath.

This is disastrous, though. Gus recognized that Walter could not be easily controlled. He was already laying the groundwork to replace Walt in the meth lab. Walt knew this, but he intervened anyway. Was this a rare moment of selflessness on Walter's part? Perhaps. Certainly part of the decision stemmed from his war of wills with Gus. His ego wouldn't allow him to be completely under the meth lord's thumb. After all, Heisenberg arose in the first place because Walter was tired of living on terms dictated to him by others. But we cannot wholly discount the idea that he also did it because he cared about Jesse. There is no question the kid was important to him.

Not so important, however, that he won't push Jesse into destroying his own soul.

With Gus now confident that Gale Boetticher (David Constabile) is ready to take over the lab, both Walter and Jesse are marked men. Both are sure to be killed. The only way Walt sees to prevent that is to make sure Gus *can't* replace him – and that means killing Gale. Walt is captured by Mike before he can do it, though, leaving him to rely solely on guile. This is one of Walt's great triumphs. His apparent weakness when on the verge of being murdered by Mike is turned into a stunning trick on his part. He begs, pleads for his life, and asks to call Jesse, only to reveal Gale's location to Jesse so that Jesse can do the deed for him. The move leaves Mike powerless to act. It's one of the show's great "DAMN!" moments.

Unfortunately, it also forces Jesse to look an innocent man in the eyes and murder him in cold blood. It's hard not to be distraught at this final scene of the season. The gunshot and cut to credits left many viewers shaken, this author included. It's one of the most powerful moments of the series.

As a general rule, *Breaking Bad* can take faster jumps forward in plot development than other slow-burning shows would. (Think *The Wire*, *The Sopranos*, and so on.) This season is a prime example of that. When you look back at what takes place over the course of these thirteen installments, whole storylines that in your head lasted a season were actually just a few episodes long. The Cousins hunting Walt. Hank's search for the RV and Jesse in the hospital. Walt falling in with Gus. Jesse in rehab and falling for Andrea. Walt and Gale's working relationship. Jesse's clash with Gus. Gale's murder. In retrospect it can be a little disconcerting to consider all this took place in such a short stretch of time, because each story feels epic in its own right. Every few episodes you have a new This Is The Grand Problem for Walt and Jesse to face. And each problem is an escalation of the one before. The structure is brilliant.

This escalation is what defines the third season of *Breaking Bad.* Each action taken by Walter and Jesse takes turns they do not foresee, and each turn they take puts them deeper and deeper into situations they cannot control. This world they entered is much larger than they are. Its people more ruthless. Its rules more deadly. But now that they are in, they are in for life or death.

Because as the pair now know, if you lie with the dogs you will get fleas.

THE "I HATE SKYLER WHITE" CLUB IS MISGUIDED

Skyler White gets a bad rap in *Breaking Bad* fandom. On countless message boards she is savaged as a shrill, controlling wife who won't give poor old Walt a break. There is even a popular Facebook page devoted to hating the character. The thought seems to go, "If only she'd leave Walt alone we could see more of his thrilling adventures."

At the same time, some of these same critics refuse to forgive the bad decisions and immoral choices made by Skyler even while delighting in the bad decisions and immoral choices made by her husband.

What gives? *Breaking Bad* creator Vince Gilligan once offered his own view on the phenomenon:

> *"With the risk of painting with too broad a brush, I think the people who have these issues with the wives being too bitchy on* Breaking Bad *are misogynists, plain and simple. I like Skyler a little less now that she's succumbed to Walt's machinations, but in the early days she was the voice of morality on the show. She was the one telling him, 'You can't cook crystal meth.' She's got a tough job being married to this asshole. And this, by the way, is why I should avoid the Internet at all costs. People are griping about Skyler White being too much of a killjoy to her meth-cooking, murdering husband? She's telling him not to be a murderer and a guy who cooks drugs for kids. How could you have a problem with that?" (1)*

Whether or not this sweeping view is accurate is debatable. It's rather harsh to call an entire group of people misogynists because they don't like a television character, and in the interest of full disclosure, this author wasn't her biggest fan in the early days of the show, either. Despite her best intentions, she could be overbearing. Take, for example, that she was oblivious to the fact that Walt didn't want to undergo cancer treatments. She essentially bullied him into it despite his clear protests. So it's fair to say that our first exposure to her was not endearing.

Still, it's also beyond debate that she gets raked over the coals pretty thoroughly for her bad choices – and make no mistake, she makes plenty of them – in a way her murdering husband rarely is.

Because she was destined to be Walt's foil when it came to family matters, Anna Gunn, who plays Skyler, knew early on that her character would not be popular among fans. "As the one character who consistently opposes Walter and calls him on his lies, Skyler is, in a sense, his antagonist. So from the beginning, I was aware that she might not be the show's most popular character," she wrote in *The New York Times.* (2) The level of disdain some had for her, however, came as a shock.

How valid are the criticisms of Skyler's actions? When you break them down, it becomes clear that she is, in fact, being held to a standard we don't hold other characters to. Further, the criticism often ignores the larger context of *why* she does what she does.

Some go right back to the pilot episode to point out how shrill and controlling she appears, noting, for instance, that she scolds Walter for using the wrong credit card. All this does is skirt over the key point of the scene, which was to show the White's financial problems as well as to note that Walt was a man without focus in his life – he couldn't even be bothered to indulge in these small money management measures, after all – while Skyler held the household together.

And indeed she *does* hold the household together, and does so throughout the series, even when the heat Walt brings down on them grows nearly unbearable. The decisions she has to make are difficult in large part because she is forced to react to problems that are not of her own making. As she tells Walt at one point, "Someone needs to protect this family from the man who protects this family." While Walt flies by the seat of his pants and puts the White household in ever-increasing danger, Skyler works to hold things together in whatever way she can. After all, she can't *stop* Walt. Not without her children being taken into protective custody. So she's left to figure out how to grapple with what he does.

The biggest sin laid at the feet of Skyler White is her affair with Ted Beneke (Christopher Cousins), her boss at Beneke Fabricators. This affair is the big decision to which Skyler White haters point to display why she's a loathsome character, but in doing so they completely ignore what pushed things to that point in the first place.

Before Skyler went to Ted, the White marriage was already on unstable ground thanks to Walt's lies and seemingly irrational behavior. Skyler tried to work through Walt's increasingly erratic behavior at first, but it soon became clear that something else was going on with him. He disappeared for days, was hiding a second telephone, and had found a mysterious source of money. It's hard to blame her for starting to lose trust in Walt, given how things appeared from her vantage point.

And then came the big reveal. Walter finally admits that there was no "fugue state," no charity from the Schwartz family, no visits to his mother. Skyler finally forces the truth out of him: he has been cooking methamphetamine. Her husband is apparently a high-level criminal. This puts her over the edge; now she wants to get her drug dealing husband to leave the house and take his dangerous trade away from the children, a perfectly reasonable desire by any objective measure. He refuses. And only then, in the face of being unable to get rid of her meth dealing husband, does she sleep with Ted Beneke.

Did she do it to seek comfort in another man's arms? No. The key to unraveling the motivation behind the affair is this: She *immediately* tells Walt about it. She goes to Ted knowing that Ted desires her, invites a liaison, and then goes straight home to tell Walt, "I fucked Ted." Why? Because the point wasn't to have an affair, it was to get the drug manufacturer away from her children. It was to hit him with a blow so hard that he'd have no choice *but* to accept that things were over. Walter's version of protecting his family placed them in danger. Skyler's was to push the *real* danger out of the household.

Much of the audience can abide Walt destroying lives, engaging in murder and selling a dangerous drug – he's charismatic and entertaining, after all – but Skyler's affair is beyond the pale. That's preposterous. Her decision is certainly not a morally pure one, but taken in context it's understandable why she did what she did.

As the money starts to roll in her moral purity continues to be tainted, both as a result of her ongoing relationship with Ted as well as through her choice to abandon her efforts to drive Walt away, but again, protecting her family is the driving force behind her decisions. Skyler does not go on shopping sprees with the stacks of cash Walter is taking home. She does not live a better, more luxurious life because of it. In fact, she (smartly) reins in Walt on his spending. She recognizes that the money will expose them to attention from the authorities, thus fragmenting their household and upending their kids' lives, and so she does what she has always done: she sacrifices for the benefit of her family, losing a little piece of herself when she agrees to launder the money Walt is bringing home.

This morally impure decision – something Skyler White haters often use as proof that she's not a good person – might have saved her entire family.

So, too, does her decision to give a large chunk of that money to Ted Beneke. Ted owed a big debt to the IRS, a debt he could not afford to pay, so Skyler gives him the money needed to settle up. The whole point of her giving him that money – and this was made explicit many times – was that if Ted was investigated then the Whites would be audited, too. If audited, their money laundering, and by extension the source of that money, would be found out. It's why she got involved in the laundering in the first place. Because she knew her family would be exposed if it wasn't done properly. Walt put her in a position where she felt the best choice for the family was for her to act.

This is the dilemma Skyler White is put in repeatedly. She is forced to choose between getting out of the way and letting her family face the fallout of Walter's increasingly poor decisions, or to step in, do what has to be done to minimize the damage even at the cost of her own moral purity, and lose a little more of herself each time she does.

In some ways, this is another of the show's great tragedies.

Critics ask why she doesn't just turn Walt in, but if things were that easy in the world of *Breaking Bad* she'd have done so long ago. What could she have done different? Even she realizes that the answer is "not much." As she says in season 5's "Fifty One":

> *"I don't have any of your magic, Walt. I don't know what to do. I'm a coward. I can't go to the police, I can't stop laundering your money, I can't keep you out of this house, I can't even keep you out of my bed. All I can do is wait. That's it, that's the only good option. Hold on. Bide my time. And wait."*

Skyler acted to keep a drug dealer out of her house, and later to keep the feds out of her house. She acted to keep danger away from her family, and then, after the Whites decided they'd pretend to have a normal life, to keep the feds from shattering things to pieces. None of these decisions were morally untainted, but all were made for selfless reasons. Her reward? In the end she was left a shell of a woman, alone in a dark apartment, chain smoking, hollow, the sacrifices she made unrecognized and thankless. However misguided some of her choices may have been – and they were – she destroyed herself to ensure her family was not destroyed.

For this, a loud minority of fans hate her.

If only we held Walter himself to such standards.

1) Vulture, "Vince Gilligan on the End of Breaking Bad," May 12, 2013

2) The New York Times, "I Have A Character Issue," August 23, 2013

INSIDE THE MIND OF GUSTAVO FRING

"What does a man do, Walter? A man provides for his family. And he does it even when he's not appreciated, or respected, or even loved. He simply bears up and he does it. Because he's a man." –Gustavo Fring

Gustavo Fring. A successful businessman respected by the law enforcement community for his support of their efforts. A gentle, noble man who works hard and treats others well.

That was, at least, how the world saw him prior to the revelation that he was a drug lord.

The real Gus Fring (played with gravitas by Giancarlo Esposito) was more complex than that. Noble and businesslike in his own way, yes, but also ruthless, driven, and possessing a keen eye for what will give him the upper hand in any situation, this powerful crime lord was driven less by greed than he was by the gaping emptiness of loss. That is, perhaps, why he will always be *Breaking Bad's* most memorable, imposing, and important villain other than Walter White himself.

Gus was charming, in some ways the most classically charming character on the show, but he was not a good man. He regularly ordered people killed when it suited him, was boss of people who both used children for murder, and even committed cold-blooded murder with his own hands. You believe he is smart and honorable when you first meet him – there is an air of charisma and sophistication about him even when dressed in a fast food uniform – but he's not honorable. Not when it doesn't serve his purposes. He's *ruthless.* When coupled with his brilliant mind, he serves as the ultimate foil for Walter White and one of the few who can match him move for move.

What makes Gus compelling, however, is not merely that he is a worthy match for Walt. Rather, it's that Gus contains hidden complexities that are only hinted at but which give him a richness few other television villains can boast.

Key to all of this is that Gus is motivated largely by loss.

Gus was born in Chile before emigrating to Mexico, and then to the United States. His Chilean past is an enigma, though there are vague hints that he was wrapped up in nefarious doings, perhaps as part of the notorious Pinochet regime. His involvement is never made clear, and all records of him as a Chilean citizen are gone. Neither Mike nor Hank, the show's two most capable investigators, are able to dig up anything about his time in Chile. The only thing we know is that Gus is more than he seems.

Once in Mexico, he partners up with Maximino Arciniega (James Martinez), a chemist, and they start a chain of chicken restaurants which they use as a cover for a methamphetamine production operation. Their idea is to maneuver the local Cartel lord, Don Eladio (Steven Bauer), into a meeting in the hopes of pitching a partnership with him. Their plan works. They get their meeting.

It doesn't go well.

Gus and his partner deceived their way into Don Eladio's presence. Rather than find their ruse clever, he finds it insulting. He feels that their ploy disrespected him, so he has one of his key henchman, Hector Salamanca (Mark Margolis), shoot and kill Maximino as Gus watches. Gus himself is left alive because, as Don Eladio tells him, "I know who you are. But understand, you are not in Chile anymore."

Maximino's murder is a terrible blow. In one of the show's most memorable images, Gus lays on the ground next to Don Eladio's pool, his face contorted in pain and disbelief, as he watches his partner's blood drain into the pool. He is shattered by this. Broken. This one moment, this lesson by the crime boss, becomes the key event in Gus's life (until he meets Walter White), an event that silently motivates him to cooperate with the Cartel, build an empire, and then use that empire to destroy the very people who took Maximino from him.

Why does this one death affect Gus so much when the Gus we meet does not blink when his business associates die, and in fact has no qualms about killing them with his own hands when necessary?

Perhaps because Maximino was not merely a business partner. Perhaps because he was also Gus's lover.

This is, of course, mere speculation. Vince Gilligan and Giancarlo Esposito both decline to be specific about Mr. Fring's orientation, saying they prefer for the audience to decide for themselves, though Gilligan does say it's likely the case. "I think they probably were lovers. And therefore it was understandably a very crushing, terrible loss for Gus, one that he would never forget. That one bit of emotion that he allowed himself ultimately proved to be his undoing." (1)

Even if not spelled out in the show, the notion seems an obvious one. Gus has no family that we can see. He briefly mentions "the children," which leads us to believe he has a family off camera, but in retrospect we wonder if he meant "the children" in a general sense. (He was talking to Walt about diet preferences when he said it in season 3's "Abiquiu".) Being an older single man without family means nothing, of course. It's the way in which Maximino's death bore right into Gus's soul so strongly that Gus spent years waiting for, planning and executing his revenge that leads us to believe their relationship went beyond business.

This is especially compelling because *Breaking Bad* makes the brilliant choice to just not deal with the question at all. Gus's sexuality was a major plot point without it ever actually being a major plot point, if you can understand that twisted logic. It just ... *was*. It was treated like you'd treat any relationship. No need to explore it any further, nor even to make a special point of acknowledging it beyond cinematic language telling us something more was there between them. The show never came right out and said Gus and Maximino were lovers, but it didn't need to. The most important thing wasn't the relationship, it was the way Max's murder burdened Gus.

This willingness to trust the audience is one of the hallmarks of the show, and is one of the reasons why Gus is such an effective character. In some ways, despite his ruthless behavior and the fact that he stands in the way of a character we enjoy watching, we pity his loss. He is not alone in that. Many of the very best villains of cinema are noteworthy in part because we *don't* really hate them, and in fact have some degree of pity for them. *Psycho's* Norman Bates, tortured by the memory of his awful mother. Gollum/Smeagol of *The Lord of the Rings*, twisted by the crippling allure of the One Ring. Roy Batty of *Blade Runner* and that glorious final speech:

"I've seen things you people wouldn't believe. Attack ships on fire off the shoulder of Orion. I watched c-beams glitter in the dark near the Tannhäuser Gate. All those moments will be lost in time, like tears in rain."

And there are many others. The great villains of the screen, whether in cinema or television, are more than mustache-twirling clichés, they are nuanced, complex characters with as much depth as the heroes they antagonize.

That, along with the immense charm Giancarlo brings to the role, is why Gus was such a brilliant character. That glimpse into his past gave him layers of humanity that made him compelling in a way other TV bad guys aren't. He's a different kind of complex than Walt. Walt *lies* to himself about his motivations, but it's clear to the viewer that his whole "I want to support my family" justification is a farce. With Gus, on the other hand, there is no ambiguity in his motivations both for the audience and for himself. He knows exactly who he is and what he is capable of. The man was a remorseless murderer who killed for selfish reasons.

Yet we can't help but be drawn in by him, and not simply because he's such a charming man. Rather, it's because his selfishness is not rooted in greed or a flawed ego that needs massaging, but in something we can all relate to: lost love.

1) Entertainment Weekly, "'Breaking Bad' creator Vince Gilligan talks about That Scene from the season finale," December 18, 2011

BREAKING DOWN SEASON 4

This is, to put it in crude terms, where the shit hits the fan. Here, Walter and Jesse have their final confrontation with the series' primary antagonist, Gus Fring. Their actions at the close of season 3 left them in a massive, sticky web. It's either find a way to break free or die.

Which is easier said than done.

The fourth season picks up from the very moment the third left off. Walter is in captivity, held by Mike and Victor (Jeremiah Bitsui), one of Gus's most trusted men. But Jesse has just killed Gale Boetticher, ensuring that Gus cannot have the pair killed without losing his very lucrative blue meth business.

Observe that other than tie up the loose ends from season 3's finale, the primary thing the fourth season opener accomplishes is to hit the reset button, essentially putting us back to the Walt And Jesse Cook For Gus status quo – but with ten times more tension than before. Jesse and Walt are partners again, they are working for Gus again, but they are constantly walking on eggshells. Gus does not trust them. They do not trust him. And all parties know that if given the chance, one would murder the other at the drop of a hat.

It's almost exactly the situation we just left, but now with an ominous shadow hanging over it all. Pretty neat trick for Gilligan and the gang to pull that off.

That status quo can only last so long, however. The entire arrangement is a house of cards, and the air is getting breezy. By this point Gus regrets ever having gotten involved with Walt. (Doesn't everyone?) Gus's problem is, he has no good way to replace him. Gale is dead. He has no trust in Jesse. And he was forced to kill the only other guy who knows Walt's formula, Victor, after Victor was seen at the site of Gale's murder. This last thing is a messy bit of business Gus performs in front of a stunned Walt and Jesse in part to clean up a problem and in part to send a message to them.

The message is sent. Walter realizes the only way he and his family, along with Jesse, will escape this situation alive is if he kills Gus. With the ever vigilant Mike standing in the way, however, his chances seem slim. Walt purchases a gun and repeatedly tries to set up meetings with Gus, but Gustavo Fring did not get into the position he's in by being incautious. He knows Walt is a danger and keeps him at arm's length.

Meanwhile, Walt has another problem. Jesse is collapsing into a chaotic state of recklessness and drug abuse. His house is filled with people he doesn't even know. He spends money with carelessness that can expose the entire operation. It gets to the point where Walt, Mike, and Gus are all seeking ways to rein Jesse in.

At the same time, Gale Boetticher's murder draws the attention of local police, who bring Hank into the investigation because of possible ties to meth. Through this, Hank begins to put more pieces of the Heisenberg puzzle together. A notebook found in Gale's apartment seems to tie him to a major meth-making operation, and clues in that notebook cause Hank to wonder if there is a connection between "Gale's" meth operation and Los Pollos Hermanos, the fast food chicken chain Gus Fring uses as a cover for his meth empire. Soon, Hank begins to think he has found his Heisenberg in Gale. All the evidence points to it.

Walter may be in a position to cut some of these problems off at the pass, but in order to do so he has to overcome his own failings, and that doesn't come easily. When Hank praises "Gale's" product in front of Walt, Walt is so bothered he almost blows his cover by suggesting there was no way Gale could have worked alone. Walt takes tremendous pride in his product. It is, in a twisted and sad way, his life's greatest work. He wasn't going to let Gale get the credit. In refuting Hank's praise, Walt places the seeds of doubt in Hank's mind that Gale may not have been Heisenberg after all. In turn, this reignites Hank's investigation.

Now, of course, Walt is caught in the middle of Hank's renewed interest in Heisenberg. Hank maneuvers to uncover the truth about Gus, and he recruits Walt to help him. Meanwhile, Walt is trying to get Hank off Gus's trail even as he tries to figure out a way to kill Gus. On top of that, Gus sets into motion a plan to replace Walt, with Jesse as the pawn. It's a mess. These moves typify this entire season, which is made up of a series of chess pieces being slid into place. Move, countermove, move, take a piece, all working towards a moment when both the black and the white king are on the verge of being placed in checkmate (as we see in a season 5 callback). The question is who will get there first.

Gus's strategy is unexpected. What if he can turn Jesse against Walt? He doesn't respect the young man, but he sees his usefulness. However, he underestimates Jesse's strict moral code – under no circumstances will Jesse let Mr. White be killed, even though by this point he doesn't trust the guy – but he correctly surmises that Jesse is now capable of running the meth lab on his own. This may be an opportunity for Gus to solve many problems all at once. Gus, you see, has long harbored resentment for the Cartel. He was wronged by them many years prior (see "Inside the Mind of Gustavo Fring") and has since sought an opportunity to exact revenge. He'll find it in Jesse. The Cartel wants a piece of Gus's blue meth operation, and after a few tense standoffs, Gus decides to give them what they want.

Or so it appears.

Gus, Mike and Jesse go to Mexico, where Jesse will teach the Cartel's men how to cook the ultra-pure blue meth that has made Gus's southwestern U.S. empire so profitable. While there, Gus stages a daring coup, taking down Cartel head Don Eladio and all his men. In one fell stroke, Gus has his revenge on Don Eladio, his meth cook, and his independence from the Cartel, which without a leadership structure is now left in shambles. All that is left is to take care of Walt.

Walt knows something is coming. He can see the writing on the wall. Gus will replace him with Jesse, and he and his family will be killed. He scrambles to get them out of town via a connection provided by Saul Goodman, a "disappearer" who will give the Whites a new life, but at the last moment Walt discovers that he can't pay the connection because Skyler gave the money to Ted Beneke. She did so with the best of intentions – Ted needed to pay back taxes to the IRS or risk being subject to an investigation, and that investigation would cause the authorities to look into the Whites, too, thus revealing their money laundering scheme – but good intentions have a way of turning on you, particularly in *Breaking Bad.*

From here it's a race. Walt has to find a way to kill Gus. He also has to find a way to get Jesse on his side. His means of doing so is perhaps Walt's most sinister deed yet. Vince Gilligan and his team decide to test the limits of the audience's trust by having Walt execute an elaborate plan entirely off-screen, and never actually telling us that Walt is executing the plan. Even more, the plan is one that makes us lose any remaining sympathy for Walt: he poisons a child.

Walter knows Jesse cares for Andrea and Brock, the young woman he met in rehab and her son. Perhaps he can use them to turn Jesse to his side? He does so first by snatching away a vial of ricin he gave to Jesse, originally intended to be used on Gus, then by poisoning Brock with Lily of the Valley, a common plant that gives its victim flu-like symptoms, the same as ricin but not fatal if caught early. We never see this take place. It all happens off-screen. In fact, we only get our first hint that it was Walt in the closing shot of the season, and it's only confirmed in the final season by an offhand comment from Saul. As all this unfolds the audience is as in the dark as Jesse is. But by now Gilligan has earned our trust, so we play along. Jesse now believes that Brock has been poisoned. Walt convinces him that Gus is behind it. Jesse, too distraught to think clear, believes Mr. White's story and agrees to help him kill Gus.

They'll do so with a bang.

For years, Gus has been visiting Hector Salamanca (Mark Margolis), a former Cartel captain. We first met Hector in season two. Then, he appeared to be nothing more than Tuco's crazy wheelchair-bound uncle hammering away at a bell, ding ding ding, out of his mind but harmless. We later learn he was the brutal Cartel man who put a bullet in the head of Gus's lover and partner, Max. Gus now visits him in a care facility, taunting him on a regular basis, teasing out a long torture until the day he can exact his full measure of revenge. After his victory in Mexico, that day has come. Don Eladio and his cronies are dead. Gus has won. And so Gus goes to Hector to gloat – the only time we ever see the otherwise businesslike Gus indulge in matters of ego.

It would be a fatal mistake.

Tipped off about the visits by Jesse, Walt rigs Hector's wheelchair with an explosive device. When Hector rings his bell – that bell was already one of the icons of the series, so the decision to use it here was a stroke of genius by the writers – the explosive device will go off. Hector knows this. He knows he will die when this happens. But he also knows that Gus has destroyed his entire family and all his business associates. This? This will be Hector's one chance to snatch victory from the jaws of defeat.

And so Gus comes to gloat.

Hector rings his bell.

And the television audience gasps.

That dramatic reveal of Gus staggering from the room with half his face blown off is probably the moment during which *Breaking Bad* was finally thrust into the larger public consciousness once and for all. It's the moment it went from being that show your friends mentioned from time to time to being that show your friends *WOULDN'T SHUT THE HELL UP ABOUT.* Just as there was an explosion in Hector Salamanca's room, there was a small explosion on social media immediately after the episode aired. We were stunned not by the turn of events, but by how damn *cool* it was. By the intricacy of the plot threads that had come together for that moment. Four seasons of them! By the calm and cool of Gus even in his death throes. By losing such a great character. By Walter's brilliant means of winning, and then by the dawning knowledge of just how dark Walt had to become in order to pull it off. The show was already a cult hit and a critical darling. That explosion turned it into a true pop culture juggernaut.

This was the climax. It was the capper on a season that was about confrontation and resolution. On the coming to a close of the conflicts that prevented Walter White from pursuing his goals without obstacles or interference.

In many ways, this season finale could have served as the end of the show. The narrative arcs of Gus and Mike had been building since season 2, the Cartel conflict since season 1. Those stories are resolved with Gus's death. In almost all ways, that explosive ending satisfied the surface level story arc. Though perhaps we'd need a brief 15-minute coda, you almost feel as if the *Breaking Bad* narrative could have ended there and the audience would have been satisfied.

But the *thematic* arc of the show doesn't really come to an end. We still need to watch as Walt, the guy who thinks he "won," ruins everything and everyone around him. He has to see the consequences of his actions. He has to get his comeuppance. The climax of season 4 can't end the overall story of *Breaking Bad* because it's a *happy* ending.

And happiness is something neither Walter nor those around him are destined to have, because as we'll come to learn, even his victories are tainted with heartache.

JESSE PINKMAN, OUR UNLIKELY MORAL COMPASS

"Mr. White... he's the devil. You know, he is ... he is smarter than you, he is luckier than you. Whatever... whatever you think is supposed to happen, I'm telling you, the exact reverse opposite of that is gonna happen, okay?" –Jesse Pinkman

When it comes to characters who are fascinating to unravel, Jesse Pinkman is every bit as compelling as Walter White, and in some ways moreso.

When we first meet Jesse, he's both difficult to sympathize with and a little difficult to like. This is a young, brash druggie who deals drugs, sleeps with married women, engages in petty crimes, and, most importantly, acts like the kind of loud, uneducated street kid no sane adult wants to be associated with.

Yet somehow, he becomes *Breaking Bad's* most sympathetic character and, inexplicably, the moral compass of the show.

Credit Aaron Paul, whose portrayal of Jesse has earned him four Emmy nominations as of this writing, two of them resulting in wins (2010 and 2012). Credit the writers for reaching inside the character and discovering what truly makes this street kid tick. And credit *Breaking Bad* creator Vince Gilligan for not killing Jesse in the first season as he had planned.

At first, Jesse's role is to give Walt something to play off. Their banter and their bickering is fuel for Walter's character development, but Jesse just plays a support role. He is a slightly bumbling, not-very-bright kid who manages to frustrate Walt at every turn and not much more.

As the episodes and seasons roll by, however, we begin to learn that Jesse is more than some dumb kid. He is that, to be sure, but there is something burning inside him we didn't notice at first. A need to be accepted. A need to be loved. A need for approval. It's a need that burns so bright he begins to project it onto those around him, specifically kids. Jesse has a special affinity for children, you see, one that comes to define who he is.

But more on that later. First, we need to define who Jesse is *not.* That comes by setting him side-by-side with his partner in crime.

As discussed throughout this book, Walter White is driven by ego and pride. He's a man who is adept at creating justifications for increasingly immoral actions, telling himself he's doing bad things for good reasons when in reality he is just a small, weak man who finally found a way to feel big, tough and important. He manufacturers morals to suit his selfish desires.

By contrast, Jesse is driven by a true moral compass. It's a bit broken because he's just a young, dumb kid with addiction problems, but it's there and it drives most of the decisions he makes. He's not always smart enough to see it, and tragically, he's easily manipulated into violating this code. When he does violate it, though – and he does several times, almost always at Walt's insistence – it torments him. Unlike Walt, he not only sees the way in which his actions impact others, he generally *cares* about how they impact others.

Also unlike Walt, he doesn't care about power or control or feeling more like A Big Man, he just cares about living a carefree life on his own terms. He won't hurt innocent people to do it, either (setting aside the broader argument of whether or not dealing drugs means you're hurting innocent people). Not if he doesn't have to. Not if he's not pushed into it. His motivations are completely different than Walt's, and this frequently drives a wedge between them.

Jesse, though, lacks confidence in who he is. Even *he* only thinks of himself as a dumb junkie. Walt encourages this by constantly running Jesse down – this is Walt's own self-loathing projected onto Jesse; he feels a sense power by bringing this kid down – and this weakness makes Jesse easy to manipulate. Walt has the strength to stand up to his "betters" because he's prideful and arrogant and selfish. Jesse does not because he's humble and aspires to nothing more than doing his own thing.

It takes time for Jesse to learn who he truly is. After falling back into addiction, he drags his girlfriend, Jane, into it with him. This proves to be a terrible choice. She has deep-seated addiction problems of her own. Falling prey to drugs again leads her to introduce Jesse to heroin, and in turn leads to her own overdose and death. Jesse is shattered, enters rehab, and appears to be in a daze. When he comes out, he claims to have discovered and embraced who he really is.

> Jesse Pinkman: *You either run from things, or you face them, Mr. White.*
> Walter White: *And what exactly does that mean?*
> Jesse Pinkman: *I learned it in rehab. It's all about accepting who you really are. I accept who I am.*
> Walter White: *And who are you?*
> Jesse Pinkman: *I'm the bad guy.*

But he is wrong about himself, and it takes a child to make him realize it.

We know Jesse is a restless soul with parental issues. He is estranged from his parents due to his drug use. He attempts to return home at one point only to have it made clear that they don't want him there. For a young man with a terrible need for approval, this is crushing. It's made all the worse because it separates him from his younger brother, Jake (Ben Petry), a whip-smart overachiever who secretly smokes marijuana. Jesse wants to forge a connection with Jake, but when his parents find a joint in the house, they assume it belongs to Jesse and force him to leave. In truth, it belonged to Jake. Jesse protected him anyway, the first of several times we see Jesse looking out for kids.

Jesse's true character is underscored most overtly in "Peekaboo" (Season 2, Episode 6), one of the most harrowing and difficult episodes of the show's early run. In it, Jesse goes to a house of meth addicts to confront a couple who robbed Skinny Pete (Charles Baker). No, not merely to confront them. He's there to kill them – not because he wants to, but because Walt bullied him into doing it.

Rather than a quick, easy execution, however, Jesse finds himself in a small slice of hell. A tiny red-haired boy lives there, silent and innocent. He lives in squalor. His meth-addicted parents do little (if anything) to care for him. Jesse is horrified. It stirs something in him. Does he see some of himself in this boy? You get the sense that he does. This poor young boy, neglected, no one there for him, how could it not touch a place Jesse didn't even know he had inside him?

"It really showed the audience that Jesse has a heart, that moment where he sees the kid. And that's what's so devastating, is there are so many kids out there like that. And when Jesse saw that little boy, he knew that he had to get this kid out of there." –Aaron Paul (1)

His need to protect children – in a sense to become the fatherly protector he unconsciously wishes he had – manifests itself again in Brock, the young son of Andrea Cantillo, a woman he met in rehab. When he first meets Andrea his goal is to seduce her and then begin selling meth to her. He gets her interested in being a buyer, but quickly pulls back when he discovers she has a son. Suddenly, the very idea of her doing drugs while caring for a child enrages him. He won't allow it.

Things spiral out of control from there. Jesse finds out that Andrea's ten-year-old brother, Tomas, is the one who killed his friend Combo, and that this same boy is being used in Gus Fring's drug dealing operation. Walt struggles desperately to keep Jesse's outrage in check, but he can't do it. With no regard for his own safety, Jesse confronts the region's most powerful drug lord and demands that he stop using children in his operation. In order to keep Walt as his cook, Gus agrees – but his street level thugs kill Tomas, presumably to silence him. Jesse attempts to kill them in revenge. Walt intervenes and saves Jesse's life. Both Walter and Jesse are suddenly in Gus's crosshairs. Walt pushes Jesse to kill Gale in order to keep both of them alive.

It's a mess.

But it's a mess because Jesse's moral compass pushes him to actions that seem to work against his self-interest. If keeping children away from drug dealing and murder means his own life is forfeit, so be it. There is no conflict in his mind; no second thoughts; no grey area. For Jesse Pinkman, protecting kids is just what you *do*. The fact that he never has to pause and consider whether he's doing the right thing or the smart thing is what makes Jesse so different from Walt. Walt acts for *Walt*, none other. He puts himself first. Jesse, on the other hand, rarely considers himself at all.

Those differences are ultimately what tear them apart.

While on a heist to steal a supply of methylamine for use in Walt and Jesse's meth operation, a hired hand named Todd Alquist (Jesse Plemons) shoots and kills a 14-year-old boy who unwittingly witnessed the tail end of their robbery. Jesse is distraught by the needless murder, but is pushed over the edge when Walt actually *defends* the shooting. Later, a series of clues make Jesse realize that when Andrea's son Brock was poisoned some months earlier – something Mr. White convinced him was done by Gus, thus prompting Jesse to assist in Gus's assassination – the poisoning was actually planned by Mr. White himself.

This sends Jesse over the edge. He attempts to burn down the White household, gets talked into helping Hank bring Walt down, and the entire endgame of *Breaking Bad* is set into motion.

All because Jesse cares about the innocents caught in his wake.

It's a powerful difference between the show's two main protagonists. Jesse sees what Walter cannot. He recognizes that their actions have consequences and that those consequences often result in innocent people getting hurt. And unlike Walter, this matters to him. It's important. So important that in the end, the brash young loser we met in the first episode defies the expectations we had of him and throws away millions of dollars because it had been tainted by innocent blood. In his mind, better that than to gain at the expense of those who lead pure lives.

Through this trait, and through Jesse's reluctant realization that he's not some worthless street thug – Jesse never really figures out who he is, only that he's not the sort of person who lets children get hurt – the show becomes not just about Walter's transformation, but also about Jesse's.

And that's why the true, final, ultimate confrontation of *Breaking Bad* is not between Walt and Gus or Walt and Hank or Walt and Neo-Nazis. It's between Walt and Jesse.

1) HitFix, "Breaking Bad star Aaron Paul looks back on Jesse Pinkman's greatest hits," July 11, 2012

REGARDING MIKE

Ahhh, Mike.

Few characters hold our attention the way Mike Ehrmantraut can. Portrayed with a direct, gritty, no-nonsense approach by Jonathan Banks (earning him Emmy and Screen Actor's Guild Award nominations in the process), in a show full of people pretending to be badass he is one of a handful of *genuine* badasses, somehow managing to be intimidating and endlessly likable at the same time.

Unraveling Mike is a difficult knot to untwine. Perhaps that's what makes him such an appealing character. What we know about him and what makes him tick is sparse. He is a former Philadelphia police officer who left the force under unspecified (and apparently controversial) circumstances. He is exceedingly adept at all things criminal, relying primarily on brains but more than capable of utilizing brawn when necessary. He is fiercely loyal to those he trusts and is not a man to break his word. And he loves his granddaughter more than anything else in the world.

Oh, and he does not like or respect Walter White in the slightest.

In fact, somehow this unrepentant criminal – we may like him, but there is no mistaking him for a hero – manages to become a moral foil for Walt, a vital role in the final seasons as Walt veers ever further from our sympathies. He is a constant reminder that there *can* be honor among thieves. A reminder that criminals *can* operate with a code of conduct we can grudgingly respect, and a reminder that the increasingly unstable Walter neither shows honor nor earns our respect.

Against all odds, though, Mike does. The contrast is striking.

Mike steals. Mike murders. Yet Mike is also honorable. This is, perhaps, why we see Mike as antagonist but not as a villain. He is unquestionably an obstacle for Walter, but his machinations do not set into motion events that put our "hero" in jeopardy. He troubles Walt not because he is pursuing his own selfish ends, but because he is able to see who Walter White truly is. Long before most people realize it, Mike Ehrmantraut recognizes that Heisenberg is a farce.

In fact, though there is no denying that Mike is an unsavory person, we can't help but sympathize a bit with what motivates his actions, morally bankrupt though they may be. A doting grandfather who secretly provides for his little girl's future and who, unlike Walt, appears to be doing so selflessly rather than due to some gaping flaw in his ego? Yes, when that is who we see it is easy to overlook just how bad a person he really is. Walter repeatedly claims his every action is driven by the desire to provide for his family, but we don't believe it. With Mike, it's different. He doesn't need to keep telling everyone around him how much he cares for his granddaughter. He doesn't have anything to prove. He loves her, that's that, and he has no want, need or desire to convince anyone else of it.

It is also easy to overlook the fact that he's a murdering thug because he's just so damn *entertaining*.

Despite being a somewhat late introduction to the cast – he was only meant to appear in a single episode ("ABQ," season 2, episode 13), but the creators liked him so much they kept writing him back into the show – consider how many amazing moments he had. He quietly storms a facility filled with Cartel and efficiently takes out one thug after another. He survives a Cartel hijacking because he's smarter and more capable than they are. He gives what may be one of the top 5 monologues of the show ("No half measures"). And on and on. This is a show that rarely glorifies violence, preferring to present it as clumsy, ugly and undesirable, but Mike's scenes of violence are almost always the sort that make you sit up and shout, "Badass!"

But perhaps his best moment is not one of violence, it's a small moment that immediately precedes an act of violence.

In the second episode of season four ("Thirty-Eight Snub"), Walter invites Mike to meet him at a bar. He wants to discuss a business matter. Walt goes on to outline a plan to kill Gus and urges Mike to join him. Walt, of course, just doesn't get it; he's oblivious both to the fact that Mike has no respect for him as well as to the fact that Mike may be a criminal, but betrayal just isn't something he engages in. It's not in his nature. Walter pleads his case all the same.

Finally, Mike looks at him, does a little bit of business with his mouth, a sort of twitchy snarl – Jonathan Banks is a master of using small facial ticks and expressions to impart a sense of growing impatience or menace – and says, "Are you done?" Then he slugs Walt.

The punch, however, is not what makes the scene. That little bit of business he does, that little facial expression, is. It says more than any line of dialogue he utters in the entire span of the show. And he has *loads* of tiny moments like that.

So it's pretty easy to see why Mike is a fan favorite.

He rises from merely entertaining to a vital part of the show's key themes, however, not because he's a badass, but because of the aforementioned contrast he provides. He is an unrepentant killer in a way Walter is not. He fully understands the impact his crimes have on people whereas Walter does not. And he is the family man Walter only pretends to be.

In a twisted, convoluted sort of way, Mike Ehrmantraut is the anti-Walter White. Whereas Walter is on the surface a good man who actually has evil in his heart, Mike is on the surface an evil man who actually has good in his heart.

Leave it to *Breaking Bad* to use one of its most unapologetically criminal characters to offer us lessons on what it means to live an honorable life.

BREAKING DOWN SEASON 5 PART 1

There is a sense of inevitability to Walter White's eventual collapse. In some ways, it would almost feel like a betrayal if Walt walked away from all he had done unscathed. We know that won't happen, of course. Even after his victory over Gus in the spectacular finale to season 4, we know that whatever afterglow he basks in is destined to fade.

When this season opens, Gus Fring is gone, his meth operation destroyed and exposed to the DEA, and Walt and Jesse appear to have gotten away scot-free. Once the dust settles, the pair are ready to begin cooking again, but first they have to deal with supply issues, how they'll distribute their product, where they can safely cook, and other problems they thought they tackled some time ago. In some ways we're back to the same problems of earlier seasons, but it's an illusion. This is the end game. This is when the chickens come home to roost. Walt appears to have removed all obstacles in his path, not realizing that his biggest obstacle of all is still before him.

And it's not Hank, or Mike, or Jesse, or Skyler. It's himself.

The murder of Gus should clear the way for Walt to stretch the business in ways he never before imagined, especially once he manages to convince Mike to come on board with him. Wiser, of course, would have been to get in, make some quick cash, and then get back out before other organized crime syndicates once again become a problem.

But that's not for Walter White. He restarts the cooking operation using the same reasoning he did at the start – we just have to earn some money and then we're good, he insists to Jesse – but his motivation is clearly power and greed rather than the half-truth about taking care of his family. At this point, his arrogance runs so high he doesn't even bother to hide it anymore. His sense of confidence is blown up beyond reason.

"You asked me if I was in the meth business or the money business," he says to Jesse. "Neither. *I'm in the empire business.*"

His inflated confidence extends to the small things, too – small things that will eventually bring him down. Take his propensity for keeping seemingly insignificant mementos that he should have tossed. His "Heisenberg" hat, the watch Jesse gave him, and most significantly, a Walt Whitman book given to him by Gale Boetticher. This is a sign that his inflated sense of indestructibility is getting the best of him.

If his confidence has any benefit, it's that it allows him to think quickly on his feet and get people who otherwise would not give him the time of day to hear him out. That's how he manages to convince Mike to take part in a relaunch of the meth operation. Mike does not trust Walter. He knows Walter is destined to crash and burn. But Walt is persistent, confident, and convincing, so Mike jumps on board. (It helps that Mike has a crew he needs to pay, therefore he needs a source of income.)

Once Walt overcomes this obstacle – and he probably doesn't realize just how big an obstacle it was because Walt never quite grasps just how little respect Mike has for him – the group probably could have had a good thing going, but Walt repeatedly cuts his own legs out from under himself by failing to recognize the needs of anyone *but* himself. He doesn't see the human toll in what he does, nor does he understand that despite his deepest fantasies, he is not a puppetmaster with the world dangling from his fingertips. When slapped with this harsh reality, he responds with anger. Take, for instance, when he attempts to manipulate Jesse into staying with him after the shooting of a young boy, Drew Sharp (Samuel Webb). The distraught Jesse refuses to cave to Mr. White's pressure. Walt's resentment when Jesse won't bend to his will is palpable; he snaps, further snipping away at an already frayed relationship. (All credit to Bryan Cranston for pulling off the subtlety in these scenes: When he's obviously being a phony you can *see* it clear as day, and when he snaps you *believe* it.)

The shooting of Drew Sharp proves to be the pivotal moment in Jesse and Walt's relationship, and in a stroke of genius it comes at the end of one of the show's most thrilling, action-adventure style episodes, "Dead Freight." Through Lydia Rodarte-Quayle (Laura Frasser), a nervous, shaky woman of the corporate world who was Gus Fring's methylamine supplier, Walt is presented with the ridiculous idea of stealing 1,000 gallons of methylamine from a train. The notion is preposterous. It seems as if there is no way they can pull it off, but thanks to a brilliant idea by Jesse (one of several instances this season of Jesse showing himself to be smart and capable in his own right) it seems the crew might actually have a chance. They draft Todd Alquist (Jesse Plemons), a petty criminal working for the pest extermination company that serves as a cover for their new meth business, to assist with the heist.

"Dead Freight" is one of the *Breaking Bad's* highlights and really underscores what makes this a brilliant show. The setup contains important character development, most notably in showcasing Jesse's moral grounding and his growing confidence and smarts. He comes up with the plan, after all, and insists that Lydia not be murdered as Mike intended. There are key developments in Walt and Skyler's relationship. And we see just how dark Walt is willing to be when he manages to look Lydia in the eye and yet still agrees to let Mike kill her (a fate Jesse helps avert).

Then it's just a rollicking fun heist episode with an exciting and tense theft sequence.

Then it does what this show does so well, which is to shock the audience and create ripples that will turn into tsunamis. You think you're watching a brilliant heist in action, but in a sudden flash it turns into the moment that splits the group apart and drives the final wedge between Walt and Jesse.

That moment comes through Todd, a latecomer to *Breaking Bad* but a character who quickly becomes one of its most fascinating. His boyish, clean-cut American appearance and demeanor mask a dead soul; a lack of empathy that makes him one of the show's more chilling villains. We're frightened of a guy like Tuco because he's wild and unpredictable, or of a guy like Gus because he's cold and calculating, but in an odd way we *understand* them. We know what they are. Todd is something alien. His eyes are dead. If they are a window to something, that something is barren and empty. He smiles. He seems pleasant. He just wants to do good work (even if that work is illegal). But he kills with the same thoughtless distance as he eats or pees. It's just a bodily function. A shrug of the shoulders, a pull of the trigger, what's the difference?

So when Drew Sharp, a young boy on a dirt bike out hunting for spiders, comes across the aftermath of their train heist, Todd draws his gun with the same nonchalance you would take out your credit card and murders the boy.

If the quick cut to credits left us breathless, the opening scene of the next episode left us numb. We watch as the crew dispose of the boy's bike and his corpse. It's dark stuff.

This marks the end of the meth business for Jesse. He won't stand by when children are murdered, and no amount of pressure from Walt will get him to change his mind. With Jesse gone, Mike leaves, too, leaving Walter alone with Todd and his "empire." The problem is, both Jesse and Mike want to sell their share of the methylamine they just stole. The idea is to cut their losses, get their cash, and get out of the business. Walt, on the other hand, is still married to the idea of being a big shot, so in a series of moves and countermoves he positions a partnership with another group of dealers that allows everyone to have their cake and eat it, too.

Everyone, that is, except Mike. Walt wants the names of Mike's associates, men Mike has been paying off from the proceeds of the meth operation, because Walt knows these men have knowledge that can sink him. Mike refuses to give up their names. Walt's infantile response is to shoot him. It's an inglorious end to the one man who instantly saw through Walter's bull and recognized him for the man he was.

After this, Walt appears to give the business a clean break. He has brought in so much money Skyler cannot realistically launder it all in their lifetime. All his enemies are gone. In a brilliant move executed with the help of a group of Neo-Nazis Todd connects Walt with, all of Mike's men are murdered in prison, eliminating the last people who could connect Walt with Gus Fring. And through Lydia's overseas connections, his blue meth is now dominating the market in Czechoslovakia, too. Walter is free to be the king he had longed to be. But he has a problem, and one that threatens to undermine all he has accomplished. No, two problems.

First, his cancer has made a sudden return.

And second, Hank has to use the bathroom.

It's the Little Things

You have to pay attention. If you don't, you might miss something. This becomes clear after multiple viewings of *Breaking Bad.* Mercifully, we don't mean that in the way it applies to a show like *Lost*, where you have to keep a spreadsheet of the details in order to piece together unclear aspects of the narrative. Rather, we mean to say that one of the true delights and wonders of this show is that its brilliance is built not of a few large things, but of many small things. Here are a few of them.

The Comedy

Breaking Bad was one of television's most powerful dramas, which makes it perhaps surprising that at times it could also be one of television's *funniest* shows. But it was. It was also a black comedy, intertwining serious situations with absurdist humor, funny dialogue, and silly moments. This succeeded in large part because Bryan Cranston is equally adept at both drama and comedy. He can make you shudder and he can make you laugh. He's especially good at physical comedy. There are moments in Breaking *Bad* where his physicality brings to mind comedians like John Ritter. The way he flails as he throws pizza onto his garage roof or gets tangled up in phone cords, this is physical comedy worthy of a silent movie. Couple that with liquefied bodies crashing through ceilings, ridiculously immature sidekicks, over-the-top lawyers, huffing and puffing bodyguards and Aaron Paul's relentless energy, and it becomes clear that humor is one of this show's unheralded heroes.

The Uneasy Anticipation

Cliffhangers are cheap and easy, but *Breaking Bad* rarely resorts to the cheap and easy. Instead, it builds a narrative that has you on the edge of your seat wondering how Walt will worm out of his latest jam. That uneasiness is made worse because the other half of the time you're thinking, "Walt, you're a dickhead. I hope someone knocks you out." The show manages to balance these traits to keep you coming back again and again, whether you're waiting a week between episodes or watching them in a marathon.

The Stunning Direction

Vince Gilligan, Bryan Cranston, Aaron Paul and others deserve their accolades, but another big hand needs to be given to the cinematographers and directors who gave this show a visual presentation usually reserved for a Hollywood feature. The staging, camera work, and shot composition seen in *Breaking Bad* were consistently head and shoulders above almost any other show you can name. These weren't multi-camera TV directors who half-assed it to stay on schedule and under budget. They went the extra mile to make this show beautiful, as evidenced by stunning time-lapse shots, creative camera angles, artistic shot composition, and editing with an attention to enhancing the scene.

They Trust Us, We Trust Them

Few shows are willing to trust the audience to come along on a ride with them like *Breaking Bad*, and even fewer shows are willing to trust the audience's intelligence to the extent this show does. In return, we give Gilligan and his crew our trust, knowing that they're going to deliver on their promise of providing smart entertainment. One of the prime examples of trusting the audience to trust them comes in Walt's poisoning of Brock. Walt uses a common plant to poison the boy, but the entire act takes place off screen. Initially, we only know he did it because the camera lingers on a potted plant in Walt's backyard at the close of season 4. The show trusts us to put the pieces together. How he pulled it off is a mystery. Later, a few stray lines of dialogue tell us that he has Saul help him, but again, the details are unclear. And you know what? They don't matter. By this point we trust Gilligan, and in turn he trusts the audience to play along. It's a wonderful bit of mutual respect that resonates throughout the show.

The Tantalizing Hints & Blown Expectations

When *Breaking Bad* teases, it teases well and turns your expectations on their head. The obvious example is the teddy bear and debris of season 2. These clues seemed to make us think Walt and Jesse were going to be busted, but the truth was something out of left field. An example less talked about came in the form of graffiti. In the final season, Walter White returns to his house to find it gated in and abandoned. Inside, the word "Heisenberg" is spray painted on the living room wall. The "Heisenberg" on the wall makes it clear he has been outed, but it doesn't mean he got caught – he obviously didn't – nor does it say who outed him. So who did it? It's a hint that seduces us into watching more, especially because we know it's unlikely to signal what we think it signals. Defying expectations in this way became a hallmark of the show, making it as unpredictable as television can be.

And without question, that's part of why we loved it.

It's Still The Comedy

For all its tension and drama, sometimes *Breaking Bad* indulges in scenes that are absurdly comedic. Take season 4's "Bullet Points," for example, and the scene during which Skyler is coaching Walt on the story they're going to tell Hank and Marie in order to explain away the White's sudden influx of cash. The interaction between Walt and Skyler as they go through Skyler's script is sharp and funny, writing as good as you'll find on any other show. Walt chaffing at his lines, complaining about what he's being asked to say ("Why two terriblys?"), poking fun at Skyler. It's hilarious yet realistic time, the kind of scene that could have been plucked from a comedy and yet feels completely at home in a drama about crime and murder.

Whoa, It's The Music

In season 5's "Gliding All Over," a montage depicts Walter's meth business during its growth from a regional operation into an international business. As this montage plays out, we listen to "Crystal Blue Persuasion," a 1969 song by Tommy James and the Shondells. This glorious scene was a picture-perfect marriage of visuals and song, but more than that, it served as the most inspired example of something the show had long done: picked great music to accompany its on-screen action. From the original score work of Dave Porter to the impeccable song choices, when it came to music, *Breaking Bad* excelled.

No Detail Is Wasted

A lot of shows that invent on the fly – and let's be clear, virtually all episodic television is made up as the show goes along – make it pretty *obvious* they're inventing on the fly. Not this show. *Breaking Bad* manages to pull elements from the archives and weave them back into the show and have it feel totally organic and natural. Stuff can pop up from two or three seasons prior and it never feels forced. Who could have imagined that Tuco's strange bell-ringing uncle would play such an important role in the show, or that Gale's love of Walt Whitman would factor into Walter White's undoing? In *Breaking Bad*, everything matters. Nothing is wasted. You never know when that one small thing will become vital to the narrative. The sum total of all this attention to detail is something wonderful. After five seasons of amazing television, you feel as if you have watched a meticulously planned saga outlined down to the smallest detail. The truth is quite the opposite, but the ability of Gilligan and his team of writers to ensure that no detail is wasted make it seem otherwise.

The Nobodies

Much has been said about the main players and supporting cast of *Breaking Bad* – this book is just a drop in the bucket when it comes to such commentary – but less is said about the bit players who make fleeting appearances and then are gone. Take a waiter from the show's final season as a prime example. Walt and Skyler are meeting Hank and Marie in a restaurant. Walt is about to pull off a cunning stunt to keep Hank off his trail. And at this terribly tense dinner, they have an enthusiastic, chipper waiter who initially seems oblivious to the tension in the air. A small moment and a small character, yes, but they add up. The undercover cop who arrests Badger. The pompous douche who annoys Walt into an act of arson. The receptionist at Beneke Fabricators. And so many more. These nobodies may not *matter*, but they enhance the show in immeasurable ways.

The Subtle-Yet-Potent Lines

Someone has to protect this family from the man who protects this family. Tread lightly. No more half-measures, Walter. One of the most compelling aspects of *Breaking Bad's* dialogue (already praised in a previous chapter) is that the lines with the most power are often the most understated.

The Economy

This show is *tight.* There are very few wasted lines. Very few wasted moments. Very few wasted episodes. Other shows that exist in the upper echelon of great dramas, shows like *The Sopranos, Deadwood, Lost, The Wire, Mad Men* and others, these shows were brilliant for many reasons, but even they succumbed to the occasional bout of filler material. The closest *Breaking Bad* ever came was season 3's "Fly," and even that episode provided important insight into Walter's character. With *Breaking Bad*, you can be sure that every episode matters.

No, Really, It's The Comedy

There is a reason we keep returning to this point. Moments of levity are truly woven into the show's DNA, so much so that they cannot be escaped even after it has plunged into its darkest, deepest, most dramatic waters. By the time season 5's "Buyout" comes around, the show has plumbed the depths of true horror. This episode opened, after all, with the disposal of an innocent young boy's corpse. There is very little to smile about at this point of the narrative – and then Jesse has dinner with the Whites, and suddenly we're laughing and cringing at the same time. That dinner scene, during which Skyler's utter disdain for both Jesse and Walt is tangible, Walter's need to assert dominance over Skyler is off-putting, and Jesse's feeble attempts to act casual despite the awkward situation is cringe-inducing, is as funny a scene as you'll see. That is happens during this dark hour borders on courageous.

MOTIVATION vs. JUSTIFICATION: WHAT REALLY DRIVES WALTER WHITE

"You clearly don't know who you're talking to, so let me clue you in: I am not in danger, Skyler. I am the danger. A guy opens his door and gets shot, and you think that of me? No! I am the one who knocks!"
—Walter White

Walter White is adept at many things. At chemistry. At garnering undeserved sympathy. At manipulating others. And most of all, at lying – especially to himself. His biggest lie of all is insisting that he did what he did in order to provide for his family.

The truth is that in providing this reasoning for the course he set for himself, he is merely creating an elaborate justification for he does. His true motivations lie much deeper beneath the surface.

When it comes to marriage, they say a man is only as faithful as his opportunities. Whether that is true or not, this much *is* true: when it comes to Walt and morality, he is only as noble as his opportunities. Though he played the role of an ordinary family man and working stiff before turning to crime, he had long harbored an unseen dark side unknown even to himself. Heisenberg was lurking there, waiting to be released. He just needed a trigger. He got it when he was diagnosed with inoperable lung cancer. That cancer opened the door to Walt indulging in his darker side because by that point he had nothing to lose. In a sense, he was free.

But Walter is as adept at lying to himself as he is to others, perhaps even more so, and so arose the fiction of providing for his family. Not consciously. Only at the end could he finally come to grips with what he truly was. Yet it was a fiction all the same. Creating that fiction became his first small step into darkness. From there, each step became easier than the last. Bad decisions can spin out of control for any of us, but Walt's journey also displayed that he was willing to take things further than normal people.

Such as letting a girl choke to death when he has an opportunity to save her because letting her die suited his interests.

In some alternate universe, you and I might make the initial decisions Walt did. We might break the law in order to chase easy money. But at some point we'd pull back and say, "Whoa. This is too much for me. I can't do these things. I can't be this person."

Walt doesn't, and that's because he had this in him all along. Even before "Heisenberg" reared his ugly head, Walt was prone to lashing out. Consider the perpetually *angry* and frustrated state he is in during those early episodes. He blackmails Jesse into working with him, casually sets someone's car on fire simply because the guy is a jerk ("Cancer Man," season 1, episode 4), rages at his car wash job, and more, all before fully assuming the Heisenberg mantle. Further, note how sexually aroused he becomes once he starts to do crime. Even if only subconsciously, this is a man who had been waiting his whole life to indulge in no-rules behavior. All he needed was a reason. The cancer gave him that reason.

The question is, why? Why was Walter's ego so frail? What triggered his deep dissatisfaction in what appears to be a rather idyllic middle class life?

The answer lies in the tiniest of plot threads: Gray Matter.

Years prior to becoming a family man and teacher, Walter White was a young, brilliant chemist dating the future Gretchen Schwartz (Jessica Hecht). The pair, along with their mutual friend, Elliot Schwartz (Adam Godley), formed Gray Matter, a small pharmaceutical company. Before the company could really get off the ground, however, Walt inexplicitly left Gretchen and walked away from the company, taking a buyout of $5,000. Why Walt left her is not shown on screen – the show only reveals that while away for the weekend with Gretchen and her family, Walt gets in a mood, packs his bags, and for no discernible reason leaves – but his decision to do so drove Gretchen to Elliot and drove Walt away from the company. In the years that followed Gray Matter went on to tremendous success. Elliot and Gretchen married, and Gray Matter's booming business made them millionaires many times over.

Walter, meanwhile, became a school teacher who could barely make ends meet.

This was a bitter pill to swallow. In his mind, he took credit for a great deal of the company's success and felt he never got his due. The world owed him some of the success they enjoyed, and he seethed at being denied it. This was compounded by something that never made it to screen: Walter's feelings of inadequacy when spending time with Gretchen's wealthy family.

> *"Vince Gilligan told us exactly what went down between the characters off screen: We were very much in love and we were to get married. And he came home and met my family, and I come from this really successful, wealthy family, and that knocks him on his side. He couldn't deal with this inferiority he felt — this lack of connection to privilege. It made him terrified." –Jessica Hecht (1)*

Though it never made it into a script, this is perfectly in keeping with the Walter White we came to know. He is prideful and insecure, and that pride and insecurity often get the better of him. Even something as simple as Hank giving Gale Boetticher credit for the blue meth triggers something in Walt, a knee-jerk reaction that almost causes him to blow his cover.

Exacerbating these problems is the fact that Walt never really came to understand just how broken a person he was, nor how capable of evil he was. Those around him had self-awareness. Gus understood that he was a man capable of doing bad things. Mike knew he walked on the wrong side of morality. At one point Jesse outright calls himself the bad guy. But Walt? Walt just couldn't see it, even as he allowed himself to sink further into the web of justifications he made for himself. He didn't want to accept what he was capable of doing. It frightened him. It shook him. It made him uncomfortable. But it never *stopped* him.

Refusing Elliot's offer to pay for his cancer treatment was one of the first major red flags that not all was as it seemed with Walt. It underscored the fact that he was motivated by ego and that his concern for his family, while genuine to a small extent – at least *some* part of him really did care – was largely a charade.

But eventually, even that concern becomes a tool in his ego trip. When Skyler appears to stand in the way of his self-indulgence, he rages with frustration. If only his family would behave as he wants them to he could continue to maintain his charade. And why shouldn't they? They're his. A possession. A trophy that allows him to continue buying into his elaborate self-delusion. When Skyler sees the danger Walt is putting the family in and attempts to push him away, his reaction is not of a man who is on the cusp of losing those he loves, it's of a man who wants to "win." He has to maintain control of the ordinary life he drapes over himself as cover lest he finally face who he truly is.

That Walter did not enter the world of crime solely out of a misguided sense of need but rather because of a burning desire he did not know he had is evident by how *excited* he was after he starts down his dark road. Walter's nervous, breathless fumbling during those early days in crime at times comes across like a teenage boy's first moments touching a breast, an apt analogy when you consider how sexually aggressive he becomes with Skyler, going so far as to initiate foreplay in a room full of crowded people and then having sex in his school parking lot. That liaison was more enthusiastic than they'd had in years. When Skyler asks why, he tells her, "Because it's illegal." It was like indulging in bad behavior suddenly made him feel like a man – a good indication that his justifications for doing what he does ("I want to help my family") are just examples of him lying to himself.

Another red flag illustrating what really drove him came in the moments after Gus Fring was killed. He's on the phone with Skyler. She sees on the news that Gus has been killed and wants to know what happened. Walt does not tell her, "Everything is fine, you're safe, we're going to be okay." Instead he says, "I won." That's significant. He kept telling us – kept telling *himself* – that he had to take out Gus in order to protect his family. Inside, though, he reveled in outsmarting another brilliant man and gloried in winning a war of his own creation.

Consider how many people Walter is willing to let get hurt so that he can continue on a course he never *needs* to continue down (first because was offered a job that would pay his medical costs, then because he amassed more money than he needed, and later because his cancer went into remission). That the man who once talked about ethics has a remarkably pliable moral code, that he will descend to troubling depths to stay ahead, says a great deal about what actually drives him. He's got it all justified in his mind. He keeps finding ways to say he *has* to do what he does. To protect his family, protect his life, protect his interests. He always seems to have a reason.

But as Jesse asks him once they have amassed more money than either could realistically spend, how much is enough?

It's a testament to Walter's amazing ability to lie (and Bryan Cranston's amazing ability to deliver those lies) that even in the final week of the show many viewers still believed he was motivated by a desire to provide for his family, even though it was clear that he *liked* indulging in crime.

Only in the hours before his death does he bring himself to admit the truth to Skyler, and in turn to himself. "I did it for me," he tells her. "I liked it. I was good at it and I was really … I felt alive."

Yet by then it was too late. He had already lost everything. His family. His reputation. Even his very soul.

1) AMC Blog, "Q&A – Jessica Hecht," May 5, 2009

BREAKING DOWN SEASON 5 PART 2

In the end, hubris was always going to be Walter White's downfall. Not crazed Mexican drug addicts or meth lords disguised as fast food men or retired cops turned hitmen or wives driven over the edge with discontent. Only hubris.

Walter's working relationship with Gale Boetticher was brief. Though he enjoyed working with someone whose passion for chemistry was almost a match for his own, he wanted no part of working with a partner not of his own choosing, and in the wicked chess game Walt played with Gus Fring, Gale was merely a deftly played pawn taken out early in the game. Not, however, before that pawn expressed his admiration and respect for Walter White. In writing. In a book he gave to Walt.

Which Walt kept, in an oversight that could only have sprung from an arrogant sense of invulnerability – and which he not only kept, but kept out in the open where it could be found by his DEA agent brother-in-law.

When the first half of season 5 closed, fans were left with a moment five years in the making. After chasing the elusive Heisenberg for over a year (stretched over four and a half seasons of TV), Hank Schrader (Dean Norris) strolled into Walt's bathroom, sat down to do his business, and picked up something to read. That something was Walt Whitman's *Leaves of Grass*, and inside was a note from Gale to Walt. In a rush, the pieces fell into place. Years of clues, hints, dead ends and false trails were wiped away in an instant. Hank suddenly knew the truth. Heisenberg had been under his nose the whole time.

We had to wait a year to see the fallout. (Damn you, AMC for your crass decision to split this season in two.)

But it was worth the wait. The last stretch of the series, technically season 5 part two but feeling more like season 6, is perhaps the most tense, gripping stretch of the show – and it starts with a bang. The first episode of *Breaking Bad's* run towards the finale, "Blood Money," was masterfully directed by Bryan Cranston, but the show is stolen by Dean Norris' portrayal of the relentless DEA agent. Norris takes Hank into the most difficult waters he has been in to date, and does so with a depth of drama heretofore unseen from him. Here we have Hank coming to grips with who Walter truly is, and then a remarkable confrontation between the two in which Walt warns Hank to "tread lightly."

Hank won't tread lightly, of course. He can't. He's always been something of a bull in a China shop, a crude, rough-around-the-edge cop who often did the right thing in the wrong way. When we first met Hank he was a racist, a misogynist, and kind of a creep. Over time, however, we came to respect his instincts. When others scoffed at his instinctual leaps regarding the Heisenberg case, Hank forged forward, getting closer to the truth each time. The idea that Gus Fring could be a crime boss, for instance, was laughable. This was a local business leader and generous supporter of law enforcement. The notion that he could be behind the elusive Heisenberg meth was preposterous. Except Hank was right.

The idea that his brother-in-law was Heisenberg, though, that was something else entirely. Even Hank never foresaw that.

A rapid cat-and-mouse game follows Hank's discovery. He can't go to his superiors in the DEA yet, not without building his case first, but Walt isn't making that easy for him. Worse still, there is next to no evidence to link Walt to Heisenberg. Tracking him does no good, either, since Walt is out of the business, having stepped away once his cancer returned. Hank pushes forward all the same. As the agent begins to put a case together, Walt neuters the effort with a daring ploy: he creates a video confession in which he admits to his involvement in meth production, while also implicating Hank in the operation. This would seem far-fetched, but Hank had accepted tens of thousands of dollars from the Whites after being shot by Tuco's cousins. That adds tremendous weight to the story Walt concocts. Hank can't go forward with so loose a case without being dragged down, too, and he can't build an airtight case without solid evidence. Hank is handcuffed.

In some ways, creating this video is as dark a place as Walt goes to. He poisoned young Brock, yes, but in this case he's poisoning his *family*, albeit only figuratively. He's doing exactly the opposite of what he always claimed he wanted to do, using his closest family members as pawns with the same ease he once did with others, and he does so without remorse. At this point Walter White has few boundaries. It's a betrayal of everything he convinced himself he stood for, but did he ever *truly* stand for the principles he wrapped himself in?

Meanwhile, Jesse Pinkman is falling apart. While Hank tries to sort out the knowledge that Walt is Heisenberg, Walt tries to settle down a frazzled, frayed Jesse in the clumsiest way possible: by giving him a couple million dollars. Walter thinks that if Jesse gives what he is owed from the methylamine heist he'll be fine, but this only serves to show that he doesn't know Jesse at all. Jesse doesn't want the money. A young kid died so they could earn it. Mike died as a result of it. Why would Jesse want it? So when Walt tries to force it on him with an awkward, subtext-layered hug and empty words of solace – not to mention the outright lie that Mike is probably still alive – Jesse finally calls Walt out on his ceaseless manipulation. Perhaps the hug was a bridge too far. In a way, that hug was a strange summary of their entire relationship: part manipulation and part real; both genuine and an act. It was Walt exposing a bit of his vulnerable side while also using that genuine vulnerability to nudge Jesse towards doing what he wants. Yet Jesse has finally come to grips with the way in which Mr. White had been pulling his strings, making the hug nothing more than a grotesque personal violation. He takes the money only to toss it out, literally, into the streets of a poor Albuquerque neighborhood.

So when Hank comes knocking, asking if Jesse wants to help implicate Walter for his crimes, Jesse is ready to talk.

It took money to finally trick Walt into being captured. Money is the symbol of his success; the one thing that manages to bolster the idea that what he is doing is okay. Take that away and you take away the one way he can snub a world he thinks has failed to deliver him his due, so that's exactly what Hank and Jesse conspire to do. The pair convince Walt that his massive stash of millions buried in the New Mexico desert has been found and is about to be torched. Walt races to the scene to put a stop to it, implicating himself over the phone in the process, but when he gets there he realizes that he has been caught in a trap. Hank, DEA Agent Steven Gomez (Steven Michael Quezada) and Jesse have him in a corner, and for once he cannot escape.

Walter White, the great Heisenberg, has been taken into custody.

Only, it doesn't work out like that. A group of neo-Nazis he previously hired to do a series of jail assassinations arrive on the scene and get into a standoff with Hank and the others. Walt pleads for them to back away and leave, knowing the bloodshed from this confrontation will be horrific, but they know there is no backing away now. They also realize there is something to be gained by being here. A gunfight ensues. Gomez is killed. Hank is badly wounded, and then shot in cold blood even while Walter begs for them to spare his life. For the first time, the reality of what his descent into Heisenberg truly means hits Walt. He collapses, knowing that his deeds finally led to the ultimate sin. A family member is dead because of him. All he claimed was important, all the lines he told himself he would never cross, all the promises he made to himself and Skyler, all of it washed away in a gunshot and sprayed out onto the New Mexico desert. With that one bullet, Walter White lost.

The Nazis take his money, take Jesse, and leave Walt to sort out the pieces of what is left behind.

But there *is* nothing left behind. Skyler knows Hank was taking Walt in – Marie called to gloat the moment she got the news – so when Walt shows up at home a free man she knows something is wrong. As best as she can tell, Walt murdered Hank. She confronts him with a knife, they struggle, Walt Jr. steps in, and the farce that was their family finally collapses into a heap on the floor.

He has nothing left. Just a barrel of money that is meaningless because it's *all* he has. So Walt calls a telephone number and arranges to disappear. He's taken away to a remote New England cabin, cold and alone, wanted by the DEA and no one else, finally having met defeat. It's over.

For now.

BREAKING BAD'S TEN MOST MEMORABLE MOMENTS

The idea of selecting the greatest moments of a show *filled* with memorable moments is, admittedly, like asking to be slapped around for how absent-minded you are. Such a list can only ever spark a flurry of "how could you forget Moment X?" comments from readers. Still, it's worth revisiting these scenes not only because it's fun to roll a mental highlight reel, but because many of them distill the essence of *Breaking Bad* down to a few memorable minutes. Yes, there are some that were painful to leave off – Gale's murder and Hank's shootout with the Cousins spring immediately to mind – but you have to cut things off somewhere. Taken as a whole, these moments, two from each season, serve both as an overview of what made this show so special while also just being damn good television.

The Bathtub Scene
Season 1, "Cat's in the Bag..."

Considering how dark the show eventually became, it's easy to forget that *Breaking Bad* essentially began life as a black comedy. There were grim moments of seriousness, yes – it's clear early on that this show won't compromise when we see Walt strangle Krazy 8 in Jesse's basement – but there is also an air of absurdity in those early seasons that is hard to ignore. The banter between Walt and Jesse is often hilarious, and there is a borderline slapstick element in the physicality both bring to the screen (especially the clumsy, hard-luck way in which Bryan Cranston portrays pre-Heisenberg Walter White). No scene typifies this as well as the infamous bathtub scene.

After Walt is forced to poison a drug dealer intent on killing him and Jesse, Jesse is forced to dispose of the body. Walt instructs him to use hydrofluoric acid to dissolve the corpse but warns him that he must use a certain type of plastic container to hold the acid and the body. Jesse doesn't listen. He dissolves the body with it in his bathtub instead. The acid then eats through the tub and the upstairs bathroom floor, resulting in a grotesque and hilarious waterfall of liquefied remains crashing through his ceiling. It's sick, it's demented, and it's absurdly funny – pretty much everything that defines the tone of the first season.

Walt Gives Tuco A Present
Season 1, "Crazy Handful of Nothin'"

If Walter White was anything, he was certainly resourceful. From the very first episode he showed himself capable of using his smarts to get out of a jam when he quickly concocted a poison gas to take out two drug dealers intent on killing him. In many ways this is what made Walt such an appealing anti-hero. He wasn't a badass. He was an ordinary schlep who also happened to be brilliant. And in those rare moments when he did stray into badass territory, well, he was as cool as they come.

When psychotic local drug boss Tuco Salamanca (Raymond Cruz) steals a generous supply of meth from Jesse and then hospitalizes him with a beating, chemistry teacher Walter White does the perfectly logical thing for a pasty old chemist to do: he confronts the dealer in his lair. Walt demands money for the meth that was stolen, as well as a partnership with Tuco. When Tuco balks and Walt's life appears to be in jeopardy, Walt pulls out what looks like a chunk of meth and throws it to the floor. That "meth" was actually an improvised explosive. The windows are blown out, Tuco is left in a daze, and a newly-bald Walt leaves with his money – and a newfound sense of power. It was our first glimpse of Heisenberg coming out to play, and it was badass.

Don't Call Her Skank
Season 2, "Peekaboo"

As the delightful bathtub scene showed, *Breaking Bad* was not afraid to get a little gross. Whereas that scene was played in a humorously dark way, however, a grotesque scene in the second season replaced humor with horror and in doing so served as one of the show's rare reminders that the substance peddled by Walt and Jesse ruins lives.

At the urging of Walt, Jesse arrives at the home of two destitute meth addicts only to find that they have a young child. His concern for the neglected boy puts him off his guard, allowing the addicts to take Jesse hostage. The two parents are unstable, though. When the husband's constant taunt of "skank!" finally pushes his wife too far, the wife pushes a stolen ATM onto his head, crushing his skull. The entire sequence is sickening, showcasing the depravity of the addicts for whom Walt and Jesse are producing meth, but the sound of the husband's skull being popped is what pushes it over the top. It's more than an exercise in being gross, though. The scene sets the stage for Jesse's eventual moral awakening by igniting his concern for children in neglect, making it one of the most important in the series.

Walt Just Watches
Season 2, "Phoenix"

There were hints early on that Walter White was perhaps a little more vile than we initially believed. We could almost forgive him getting into the meth business given his situation – he otherwise seemed like an affable family man, after all – but there were things that troubled us. Asking Jesse to murder people, for example, or the way he verbally and emotionally abused his partner in crime. Still, we forgave Walt his transgressions because we were entertained and we thought perhaps deep down inside he really wasn't *that* bad. Boy were we wrong.

When Jesse's girlfriend, Jane Margolis (Krysten Ritter), finds out that Walt is withholding nearly a million dollars from Jesse, she takes the kid gloves off and blackmails Walt into paying up. He does. She and Jesse then plan to skip town, but first they want to have one last drug binge. Walt shows up to try and reconcile with Jesse and finds the pair passed out from drugs. He attempts to wake Jesse, accidentally pushes Jane over onto her back, and she begins to choke on her own vomit. If she is not rolled back onto her side she is going to die. But Walt just watches. That he watches with some degree of horror only underscores the idea that he knows exactly what he's doing. This man, this *father*, watches someone's daughter die simply because he knows she posed an obstacle to him. Once Walt opens this door and steps into the darkness, there is no going back.

Skyler Pulls No Punches
Season 3, "I.F.T."

Skyler White wasn't exactly *Breaking Bad's* most popular character. While we were engrossed in Walt's increasingly dark adventures, Skyler did her damndest to steer Walt away from his darker side. When the White family started to fray at the seams thanks to Walt's erratic behavior, Skyler tried to hold things together and put a stop to Walt's strange doings. Essentially, for many in the audience Skyler White was the brooding, frowning obstacle between us and our fun. It certainly didn't help when she dropped a bomb on the guy who was (at the time) our hero.

After finding out that Walt was manufacturing meth, Skyler demanded he leave the house. Walt refused. So in an effort to drive her meth-producing husband out of the house and away from her children, Skyler chose a tactic that set fans against her once and for all: she slept with her boss, then immediately went home and told Walt about it in rather, ummm, *direct* language. "I fucked Ted" quickly became one of the most memorable lines of the show, and seeing that Skyler could be just as ruthless as Walt became one of the show's biggest gut punches.

Don't Just Stand There, Jesse
Season 3, "Half Measures"

Mr. White wasn't a particularly good or kind father figure to Jesse Pinkman, but it can't be denied that despite the regular abuse thrown at Jesse by his frustrated elder, there was a streak of genuine caring there, too. Something about the young man – what we can never be sure – triggered a protective streak in Walt.

When a horrified Jesse sought revenge on two drug dealers who first used a child to shoot his friend Combo, and then killed that same child (who also happened to be his new girlfriend's brother), the act was destined to be a death sentence, because if the drug dealers didn't kill him, their boss, Gustavo Fring, certainly would. Walt knew this, so just before Jesse walked into a hail of bullets Walt appeared out of nowhere, ran down the dealers, shot the lone survivor in the head, and commanded Jesse to run. It was a stunning moment in a show filled with them. Not only did it drop our jaws, it was an exclamation point on the growing unease between our meth-cooking duo and their chicken-cooking boss.

Walt Has a Nervous Breakdown
Season 4, "Crawl Space"

As brilliant, focused and capable as he was, Walter White was never a *calm* man. From the very first episode he was prone to fits of futile anger, clumsy frustration, and childish belligerence. Despite these failings, however, the one thing he was not prone to do was to give up. He had done that before, after all, when he gave up on Gretchen and Gray Matter. Look where it left him: with a life he hated. With the cancer giving him a deadline he couldn't ignore, giving up on reaching his goals was no longer an option. So when Walt finally cracked, he cracked hard.

Walt, realizing his days are numbered now that Gus has another way to cook Walt's blue meth, arranges to have he and his family "disappeared." All he needs to do is pay Saul's guy and the Whites can avoid being another set of numbers in Gus's body count. But as Walt discovered, Skyler gave their money away. Her intentions were good – to protect the family from an IRS investigation that would blow the lid on Walt's illicit income – but it doesn't matter. She doomed them. And so Walt lays there in the crawl space in which their money had been hidden, laughing hysterically as the camera pans up, up, up and the air fills with an ominous drone. Television is rarely this potent.

Gus as the Terminator
Season 4, "Face Off"

A case can be made that *Breaking Bad* went from a cult hit to a cultural phenomenon with this scene. That unforgettable moment was perhaps the biggest "Holy SHIT!" of the entire series. Despite the still relatively small audience at the time – 1.9 million viewers tuned in, or just 1/10th the number who watched the show's finale – the Internet exploded with glee, shock, excitement, and a wave of proselytizing from fans urging everyone and anyone to *watch this show*. For those who watched it live or without spoilers beforehand, it will likely remain one of the most memorable TV moments they ever see.

After an entire season of cat-and-mouse games between Walt and Gus, Walt rigs Hector Salamanca's wheelchair with explosives. Gus comes in to once again taunt his old adversary, but Hector is able to have the last laugh. He triggers the explosive, blowing his nursing home room to shreds. Then, unbelievably, the camera pans to the door where we see Gus strolling from the room, calm, collected, and inexplicably still alive – but only for a moment, because as the camera continues to pan we see that half his face has been blown off down to the skull. He adjusts his tie, collapses, and dies. Walt wins. The audience cheers. And the show cements its place in legend.

Wrong Place, Wrong Time
Season 5, "Dead Freight"

Breaking Bad frequently shocked us over the years, but it was never shocking just for the sake of being shocking. Even its most over-the-top moments served a greater purpose. The crash of Wayfarer 515 was a lesson in the law of unintended consequences. Murder-by-ATM underscored the reality of what meth does to people and horrified Jesse onto his path towards a purer sense of morality. Gus Fring's half-blown off face was as symbolic as it was shocking. So when a 14-year-old boy is shot in cold blood, you know it's not simply to make us gasp – even if it *does* make us gasp.

Walter, Jesse, Mike and Todd had just gotten done hijacking a train's supply of methylamine when they realize a kid on a dirt bike, Drew Sharp, has been watching them celebrate. Walt had earlier warned that no one must know about the heist, so before anyone can react, Todd shoots the kid. As an audience we were left numb, especially since the murder came at the end of a light and fun heist sequence, but not as numb as Jesse, who has an affinity for kids. The shooting ends up fracturing the short-lived post-Gus meth crew, sets the stage for Todd becoming one of the show's most hated villains, and reminds us that in the world Walter White has created for himself, no one is safe. Not even children.

Walt Offers A Friendly Warning
Season 5, "Blood Money"

We had been waiting five years for this moment. Hank, the coarse but diligent DEA agent we eventually came to respect, was destined to eventually discover that his brother-in-law was the elusive Heisenberg. The tension had long kept us on the edge of our seats, and the delicate balancing act Walt had to play to continue his role as a drug lord even while maintaining the facade of a normal family man was one of the show's greatest sources of drama. In some ways, that dichotomy defined the show. So when Hank finally found out the truth about Walter and confronted him, we expected something big.

Instead of something big and explosive, though, *Breaking Bad's* creators defied expectations and gave us a small, quiet moment more powerful than any explosion could ever be. Hank is certain Walt is Heisenberg, he just needs to build a case. Meanwhile, Walt suspects Hank is on to him, and goes to Hank's house to confront him. With the garage door down and the lights dim, the two square off, Hank seething both at Walt's betrayal and at knowing Heisenberg was under his nose the whole time, Walt not worried about being caught as much as he is about having his image as a good family man shattered. And then Walt, knowing Hank doesn't have a rock solid case yet, offers a dire warning: "If that's true, if you don't know who I am, then maybe your best course would be to tread lightly." It was heart-stopping stuff that opened the final stretch of the series with an air of menace that would last through the finale.

FINALE

Walter White made his choices. He was not a stupid man. He allowed his insecurities and ego to push him down a reckless and self-destructive path, yes, but he was certainly not stupid.

So when he decides to leave the remote New England cabin in which he has been hiding to seek revenge on those who wronged him, he knows he is destined to die.

Having lost everything else *but* his life, Walter White is okay with that.

The question leading into his final moments, then, becomes one of facing the consequences of your actions. Did Walter achieve victory in the end? Did he get what he wanted? Or did he die having failed in what he set out to do and hoped to accomplish?

It's true that in the end, Walt destroys Jack Welker (Michael Bowen), Todd and the other Neo-Nazis, saves Jesse from a life of slavery, and leaves millions to Walt Jr. It's also true that his final moves fall into place with an almost dreamlike effortlessness. Sitting in a remote New England bar while on the verge of turning himself in, the sight of his old Gray Matter partners sparks something in him, some glimpse of a plan, and so he gives up on hiding, choosing instead a suicide mission that will tie up the loose ends of his life.

It's an ending concocted by writers, yes, and as such it has a finality to it that only writers can invent. So be it. The grand question that vexes viewers and critics is not whether or not the writers provided closure to the *Breaking Bad* story – they did – it's whether or not Walter White *won.* And yes, a case can be made that in the end he achieved some measure of victory.

But if Walter White enjoys a victory, it's a hollow victory. It's a victory won at tremendous cost. Too high a cost, really. He knows it, and that's why he finally decides to go die in a rain of gunfire rather than rot away in hiding. Because that tiny victory is all he can take out of all the misery he has created.

Having purchased a machine gun from a weapons dealer he had worked with a few times before – Lawson, portrayed by Jim Beaver *(Deadwood's* Mr. Ellsworth*)* – Walt arranges to ensure his last few millions get into the hands of Walt Jr. with some creative intimidation directed at Elliot and Gretchen Schwartz, visits Skyler one last time, and then sets up a trap to kill his enemies (and himself). This will be his last hurrah.

Remarkably, it all works. He uses Badger and Skinny Pete to trick the Schwartz's into leaving his remaining money to Walt Jr. He manages to see Skyler, and during their final conversation he finally reveals what we knew all along – his actions weren't motivated by his family, they were motivated by something empty inside himself. And finally, his plan to kill Jack's crew with a trick machine gun works. The only reason Walt doesn't escape unscathed is because he accidentally catches a bullet during the climactic fire.

But how perfect is all of this, really? Some interpreted the finale to be an example of things falling into place for Walt; of Walt getting everything he wants and in the end achieving all he set out to do. Walt does kill his enemies, after all, and Walt Jr. does get money left to him. But Walt doesn't get a hero's sendoff, nor does he get everything he wanted. Walter *lost.* He lost everything he built, everything he had, and everything he would ever have. He lost his family, his dignity, any respect people had for him, his empire, most of his money, any love he experienced, his control over Jesse, and so much more.

The small victory he earned in the denouement – and that's what the final two episodes of the show were – was merely Walt getting a chance to play "If I can't win then neither can you" with Todd and the neo-Nazi crew. He had nothing left to lose, so he went on a suicide mission.

Even the last moments when he saves Jesse are tainted, because after saving the kid's life he has to face finally losing his grip on him. Note that Walt is initially there to kill Jesse along with the Neo-Nazis. Based on a news report he saw mentioning blue meth, he thinks Jesse is cooking for them. That cannot stand. Walt cannot allow Jesse to steal his (pathetic) legacy. So Jesse is on the hit list. Once he is there, however, he realizes that his former partner was just a slave for Jack and his crew, tortured daily and cooking meth against his will. When the time comes to click the button that will activate the machine gun and kill all in its path, Walt leaps forward and pushes Jesse to the ground. In the bloody aftermath, after Todd and Jack are finished for good, only the two of them are left alive. Walt slides Jesse a gun and tells him to go ahead and shoot. Kill him. It's okay. He deserves it.

Walt *does* deserve it, too. He twisted this young kid into knots. Pushed him to murder. Allowed his girlfriend to choke to death (and then told him about it just to make him hurt). Poisoned his other girlfriend's son. Set into motion events that led to that girlfriend's murder. And so much more. If anyone has earned the right to kill Walt, it's Jesse.

But Jesse refuses to do what Walt wants him to do. He instead nods, offering a final acknowledgment of all the two have been through together, and leaves Walt to die.

Jesse could have chosen to kill him, but that would have made for a tragic end for him. Part of Jesse's journey has been finding the purity in himself. It's why he became this show's moral center. Given all Mr. White put him through, Jesse shows great maturity in not murdering him. The need for that sort of revenge is small and childish and is driven by ego. It's what Walt succumbed to. It's in part what ruined him. Had Jesse done the same, his journey would have been tainted.

In many ways, leaving Walt to die alone was retribution for Jesse. It was Jesse breaking free of manipulation. It was Jesse becoming his own person. It was Jesse crawling out from under Walt's oppressive shadow. It was also Jesse finally turning his back on the dark path Walt had pushed him down. Had Jesse shot Walt when Walt asked him to, it would have been one last time in which Walt showed his power over Jesse. But because Jesse did not, he not only won the moral victory, he also retained what Walter had lost: his soul.

Still, doesn't his refusal to kill Walt when he has the chance mean that Walt gets away with all he has done?

Not at all. In fact, Jesse does the *opposite* of let him get away with it. He knows Mr. White is going to die within the hour. He sees the gunshot wound; he knows he's going to bleed out. Walt isn't getting away with anything that he hadn't already gotten away with. The only thing Jesse has to gain by killing Walt at that point is some personal satisfaction.

Jesse is beyond that now.

This brief scene – it lasts just a few moments but has the weight of six years of television viewing behind it – is a remarkably understated. And perhaps that is for the best.

So Walt is left to die with a representation of his greatest accomplishment in life: meth cooking equipment. He runs his bloody hands along the stainless steel, has perhaps the first moment of peace we see from him in the entire series, and dies.

That brief moment of contentment is remarkably sad, because look at what he has found contentment in: being alone in a meth lab, and the fact that he left blood money to a son who will be glad to learn he's dead.

If he enjoys any degree of satisfaction from this, it's a twisted, painful kind of satisfaction.

More importantly, there is no redemption for Walt in "Felina." None of what he does in that final episode excuses what he did in the 61 prior. None of it made him a hero in the end. He does not make up for his lies and crimes. He does not wash away poisoning children and destroying families and being a vile manipulator of people he claimed to care about. If we're sad that he died, it's only because we're sad the story is over.

When the terms of his "victory" in killing the Nazis and leaving Walt Jr. an inheritance (which he may never actually even get) are spelled out for what they are, it becomes clear that in the end he succeeds in nothing worth celebrating. He is forced to say goodbye to his family once and for all, has to leave behind a son (without a goodbye) who wants him dead, and is finally forced to face the reality of what his selfishness cost those around him.

He managed to snatch a small victory out of catastrophic loss, yes, but the key word is small. Walter was at peace with his death, but only because he had nothing left to lose.

Meanwhile, Skyler is a miserable, lonely woman raising a daughter who has no father and a son who sees his father as a murderer. Marie is a widow whose husband (as far as she knows) was murdered by his brother-in-law. And Walt Jr. has come to find that the man he idolized was a monster.

Is there a more miserable victory than that?

As long as the show was intent on staying honest, this is perhaps the only way *Breaking Bad* could have ended. With Walt again moving the moral goalposts in an effort to come out (in his mind) on top, but realizing much too late that his choices could only go badly.

Maybe Walt knew this all along. Perhaps he did. And so he made his choices, thinking even an inglorious death was better than death as a nameless, faceless middle class man.

CONCLUSION

For many viewers, this author included, watching those credits roll one last time was a bittersweet moment. We knew we'd never again see a new episode of *Breaking Bad.* We'd never again experience the thrill of wondering what Walter White would do next and how he would get out of his latest scrape. We'd never feel that uncomfortable sensation in our stomach as we found ourselves both drawn to and yet repulsed by Walter White.

At the same time, we knew we had just watched something special. Something that would be discussed for decades to come. We knew we not only saw great television, we also saw a rare show that was allowed to end on its own terms, giving us a self-contained narrative that actually included a dignified ending. Even better, we got to experience it alongside countless other enthusiastic fans. In a very real sense, it became a communal experience. And it was magic.

If there are lessons to be learned from *Breaking Bad*, in truth they're not the sort of lessons the average person needs to learn. Perhaps we learned a little about ourselves over this show's six years and five seasons. Perhaps we were merely entertained. As long as you enjoyed the ride – and it's hard to imagine someone *not* enjoying the ride – which experience applies to you does not matter. There was no right way to watch this show. There is no right way to interpret it. Readers are going to disagree with some things I have written in this book, some vehemently so. That's a good thing. It speaks to the complexity of the world and characters created by Vince Gilligan, Bryan Cranston, Aaron Paul and others. I welcome those disagreements, and I do so for entirely selfish reasons: They afford me the opportunity to keep talking about a show I love talking about.

And over the last several years, I have *really* enjoyed talking about it. If the act of reading a book is an act of engaging in a dialogue with the author, well, then I hope you've enjoyed talking about it with me as much as I've enjoyed talking about it with you.

Until the series premier of *Better Call Saul*...

ABOUT THE AUTHOR

In addition to being the coauthor of *A Year of Hitchcock: 52 Weeks with the Master of Suspense* (Scarecrow Press 2009) and *Hitchcock's Villains: Murderers, Maniacs and Mother Issues* (Scarecrow Press 2013), Eric San Juan is the author of *Stuff Every Husband Should Know* (Quirk Books 2011) and *Lakehurst: Barrens, Blimps & Barons* (2011), a contributing author on *Geek Wisdom: The Sacred Teachings of Nerd Culture* (Quirk Books 2011), and is the creator of the *Pitched!* series of graphic novel anthologies. He can be heard with Jim McDevitt on the official Year of Hitchcock podcast (ayearofhitchcock.com).

His writings on film, entertainment and pop culture have been featured online as well as in publications like *Weird Tales*, *Currents Magazine*, the *Philadelphia Weekly*, and others. He recently completed work on a book examining the 6,000-page graphic novel, *Cerebus*. Before *Breaking Bad* came along, he thought *Deadwood* was the greatest thing since sliced bread. He still thinks it's pretty damn good.

He can be reached at ericsanjuan@gmail.com. More information can be found at www.ericsanjuan.com.

Other Works by Eric San Juan

A Year of Hitchcock:
52 Weeks with the Master of Suspense
With Jim McDevitt
(Scarecrow Press 2009)

Stuff Every Husband Should Know
(Quirk Books 2011)

Geek Wisdom: The Sacred Teachings of Nerd Culture
With Stephen Segal, Zaki Hasan,
N.K. Jemisin, and Genevieve Valentine
(Quirk Books 2011)

Lakehurst: Barrens, Blimps & Barons:
The True Tale of a Pine Barrens Town
(2011)

Hitchcock's Villains:
Murderers, Maniacs and Mother Issues
With Jim McDevitt
(Scarecrow Press 2013)

Pitched! Volume 1: Nine Stories
(graphic novel, 2009)

Pitched! Volume 2: Seven More Stories
(graphic novel, 2010)

CPSIA information can be obtained at www.ICGtesting.com
Printed in the USA
LVOW12s1852230614

391260LV00053B/1145/P